Milton Whitney

Soil Investigations

Milton Whitney

Soil Investigations

ISBN/EAN: 9783743323278

Manufactured in Europe, USA, Canada, Australia, Japa

Cover: Foto ©ninafisch / pixelio.de

Manufactured and distributed by brebook publishing software
(www.brebook.com)

Milton Whitney

Soil Investigations

SOIL INVESTIGATIONS.

MILTON WHITNEY.

(Extracted from the Fourth Annual Report,)

MARYLAND AGRICULTURAL EXPERIMENT STATION.

REPORT OF THE PHYSICIST.

By Prof. Milton Whitney.

SOIL INVESTIGATIONS.

Introduction.

It is proposed at this time to give a brief account of the soil investigations carried on by the Station and attempt to point out the application of the results and conclusions to the explanation and solution of problems in practical agriculture.

We are glad to report that the U. S. Government has taken up this work, and, through the Weather Bureau of the Department of Agriculture, has placed a sum of money at our disposal to enable us to complete some work on hand in order to prepare a full report or monograph, to be ready for publication by next July. In view of the fact that the report to be issued by the Government will of necessity be much fuller and more exhaustive than this can be, and will contain a detailed description of the methods, formulae and data upon which our lines of reasoning are based, we will introduce into this report only such statistical and other data as will make the narrative complete—referring all who wish to follow the subject more closely and in further detail to the Government report.

It has taken six years of constant application, observation and study, in the field, plant house and laboratory, to gain a clear idea of the nature and structure of the soil in its relation to meteorology and agriculture. When, in the fall of 1890, the work was commenced here in its application to the soils of Maryland, several fundamental principles of soil physics still remained to be worked out. This required the use of very expensive apparatus, only to be found in a well-equipped physical laboratory. It was essential, also, that the work be based upon the most thorough geological data to show the area and distribution of the different soil formations. There was no reliable geological map of the State, and the Director of the U. S. Geological Survey stated that the Professors of Geology of the Johns Hopkins University had all the available data, and were themselves working out in more detail the geology of Maryland, and advised a co-operation with them in this soil work.

The work of this division of the Experiment Station on the investigation of soils was, therefore, located at the Johns Hopkins University. By permission of the Trustees of the University the work was moved in June to their large estate of Clifton, on the Harford Road, where it is at present being carried on. The reasons for this and our relations with the University are more fully set forth in the Director's report.

The President of the University and the Professors in the Departments of Chemistry, Geology and Physics have shown, from the first, an interest in the work and a cordial spirit of co-operation, with a desire to have us make a practical application of their work and information.

Argument.

It takes really very little experience for one to judge at a glance whether a soil is suited to grass or wheat or tobacco or watermelons, and he has but to turn up a small handfull of earth to see if the soil is in good condition, as regards moisture, for the growing crops. And yet, agricultural chemists have worked over this problem for years, arguing points from minute differences in chemical composition of the soils or plants, which their most refined methods make none too sure, overlooking the fact that the farmer can tell from the *appearance* whether a soil is in "good heart" and what it is best fitted to grow. The farmer cannot see these minute differences in chemical composition. He judges from the general appearance of the land, the physical structure of the soil.

Those of us who are engaged in agricultural investigations, even in soil studies, are not as far advanced as the farmer in our knowledge of the soil, nor will we be until we can understand and explain these visible signs upon which he bases his judgment. He has kept up with our work on the chemical composition of soils and has applied it and made it his own. But he goes further than we have gone, for he can tell, as no chemical means will enable us to judge, whether the land is in good condition, is fertile, has body and will hold manures, is strong or will shortly run out, is dry and leachy or retentive of moisture. He can tell what class of plants it will best produce. In this lies the key to all soil investigations. Chemical analysis has its part to play, but we have yet to get the key to the interpretation of its results. And this key is to be found in the study of the physical structure of the soil and the physical relation to meteorology and to plant growth. Meteorology has not done, and is not doing, its best good for agriculture. While we admit it is very important to have the rainfall data furnished by the Weather Bureau, still, as the rain does not benefit the crops until it enters the soil, it is very essential that the rainfall be studied below, as well as above, the surface of the ground.

Crop production is not directly limited by the amount of rainfall, but by the moisture in the soil. Six inches of rainfall a month may mean a good season, or, with this same amount differently distributed throughout the month, the crops may be injured by excessive wet or by prolonged drought. Changing seasons of wet or dry, hot or cold, have far more effect on the crops than any combination of manures.

There is a certain type of land in this State, in a certain geological formation, which is left out in pine barrens as it is too poor to put under cultivation; another type, in a different geological formation, is well suited to melons and garden truck; still other types, to tobacco, wheat and grass. This is not a matter of mere plant food. No addition of any amount or any combination of available plant food will at once enable a good wheat crop to be produced on the soil of the pine barrens, or on the light truck lands. It is a matter of available water rather than of available plant food, and if after some years the light land is brought up to produce good yields of wheat, the whole appearance and structure of the soil will be found to have changed, and with it, the relation of the soil to the movement of water—*to the movement of the rainfall after it enters the soil.*

And so in the deterioration of land, in the deterioration of our tobacco and wheat lands. It is not due to loss of plant food so much as to the causes which change the whole appearance of the soil to the eye—a change of the physical structure of the soil, a change in the relation of the soil to the movement or circulation of water.

Our work, then, is on the physical structure of the soil and its relation to the circulation of water—the movement of the rainfall after it enters the soil, and the physical effect of fertilizers and manures thereon, as related to crop production.

Summary of the Results.

This report will treat first of the underlying principles governing the circulation of water in the soil, then of the different soil types found in the State, of their structure and relation to the circulation of water, leading up to the application of these principles in a discussion of the improvement of lands. A summary will be given here, outlining the body of the report, so that it may be followed more easily.

I. The circulation of water in the soil.

a. Due to gravity or the weight of water acting with a constant force to pull the water downward, *and also*, to surface tension or the contracting power of the free surface of water, (water-air surface,) which tends to move the water either up or down or in any direction, according to circumstances.

b. The ordinary manures and fertilizing materials change the surface tension or pulling power of water.

II. The effect of fertilizers on the texture of the soil.

a. There is a large amount of space between the grains in all soils in which water may be held. The rate of movement of the water will depend: 1. Upon how much space there is. 2. Upon how this is divided up, *i. e.* upon how many grains there are per unit volume of soil. 3. Upon the arrangement of the grains of sand and clay.

b. Flocculation—a phenomenon of great importance in agriculture—changing the arrangement of the grains and consequently the texture of the soil.

III. The volume of empty space in soils.

IV. The relation of geology to agriculture.

V. Soil types.

a. Reasons for establishing soil types.

b. The very evident difference in texture is the probable cause of the difference in relation to plant growth and to local distribution of crops.

c. Soil types in Maryland and the samples from which they are made.

VI. Mechanical analysis of the type soils.

VII. Approximate number of grains per gram of soil.

VIII. Approximate extent of surface area per cubic foot of soil.

IX. The circulation of water in these type soils.

a. The relative rate of circulation of water in soils short of saturation is very different in these type soils and probably explains the difference in relation to crop production.

b. The relative rate of circulation of water in these soils when fully saturated.

c. The influence of the total volume of space.

d. The rate of circulation of water is relatively faster in light sandy lands, when far short of saturation, than in heavier clay lands, but it may be far slower in these same light lands when fully saturated, owing to the less amount of space in the soil.

X. The improvement of soils.

a. In soils having as much clay as the type requires, the grains of clay may be rearranged by causing flocculation, or the reverse, by the use of ordinary fertilizing materials.

b. In soils having less clay than the type: 1. The grains may still be rearranged, or, 2. organic matter may be precipitated from solution within the soil, in light, flocculent masses, with lime, acid phosphate, or the proper mineral manures, or constituent of the soil itself, and so fill up the spaces and retard the rate of circulation of the water.

I. The Circulation of Water in the Soil.

The motive power, which causes water to move from place to place within the soil, consists of two forces: gravity, or the weight of the water itself, and surface tension. Gravity tends to pull the water downward, and acts with a constant force per unit mass of water. Surface tension, or the contracting power of any exposed water-surface, may move the water in any direction within the soil, according to circumstances. It may act, therefore, *with* gravity to pull the water down, or *against* gravity to pull it up. This has an important practical bearing on the movement of water in sandy lands, as we shall show in speaking of the application of these principles to our type soils.

The force of gravity need not be further considered here.

Surface tension is the tendency which any exposed surface has to contract to the smallest possible area, consistent with the weight of the substance. If a mass of water is divided, or cleft in two, leaving two surfaces exposed to the air, the particles of water on either surface, which were before in the interior of the mass and attracted from all sides by like particles of water, have now water particles on only one side to attract them, with only a few air particles, comparatively very far apart, on the other side, where formerly was a compact mass of water. All the surface particles of water will therefore be pulled from within the mass of water, and the surface will tend to contract as much as possible, leaving exposed the smallest number of surface particles, and causing a continual strain or *surface tension*. On any exposed water-surface, there is always this strain or tension, ready to contract the surface, when it may.

It is a constant, definite force per foot of surface, for any substance at a given temperature. In the case of liquids and solutions, in which we are most interested, it varies with the nature of the liquid and the substance in solution.

This is *surface tension ;* and we have it in the soil as a strain or tension along the free surface of water within the soil, which tends to contract the surface and so move the water from one place to another as it is needed.

There is, on the average, about 50 per cent. by volume of space within the soil which contains no solid matter, but only air and water. This we shall call *empty space*. In a cubic foot of soil there is about half a cubic foot of empty space, but this is so divided up by the very large number of soil grains that the spaces between the grains are extremely small.

When a soil is only slightly moist the water clings to the soil grains in a thin film. It is like a soap bubble with a grain of sand or clay inside, instead of being filled with air. Where the grains come together the films are united into a continuous film of water throughout the soil, having one surface against the soil grains and the other exposed to the air in the soil. As the soil grains are surrounded by this elastic film, the tension on the exposed surface of the water will support a considerable weight, for the soil grains, thus enveloped, are extremely small and have many points of contact around which the film is thicker and is held with greater force.

If more water enters the soil the film thickens, and there is less exposed water-surface. If the empty space is completely filled with water there will be none of this exposed water-surface, and therefore, no surface tension. Gravity alone will act and with its greatest force. If the soil is nearly dry, there will be a great deal of this exposed water-surface, a great amount of surface tension, and with so little water present, gravity will have its least effect.

The grains in a cubic foot of soil have, on the average, no less than 50,000 square feet of surface area. There is less, of course, in a light sandy soil, and more than this in a clay soil. If there is only a very small amount of water in the soil the film of water around the grains will be very thin, and there will be nearly as much exposed water-surface as the surface area of the grains themselves. If a cubic foot of soil, thus slightly moistened, and having this large extent of exposed water-surface, be brought in contact with a body of soil fully saturated with water, in which there is none of this water-surface, the water-surface in the drier soil will contract, the film of water around the grains will thicken and water will be drawn from the wet into the dry soil, whether it be to move it up or down, until, neglecting gravity or the weight of water itself, there is the same amount of water in the one cubic foot of soil as in the other. When equilibrium is established there will be the same extent of exposed water-surface in these two bodies of soils.

When water is removed from a soil by evaporation or by plants, the area of this exposed water-surface is increased, and the tension tends to contract the surface and pull more water to the spot.

When rain falls on rather a dry soil, the area of the exposed water-surface in the soil is diminished, and the greater extent of water-surface below contracts and acts, with gravity, to pull the water down.

By numerous careful and verified experiments, we have found that fertilizers change this surface tension and modify the contracting power of the free surface of water to a remarkable degree, and so modify thepower which moves water from place to place in the soil.

The following table gives the surface tension of a solution in water of several of the ordinary fertilizing materials. This list is not complete, and the solutions used were of any convenient strength. The results are preliminary to give material for more thorough and detailed investigation. The surface tension is expressed in gram-meters per square meter, that is, on a square meter (or yard) of liquid surface there is sufficient energy to raise so many grams to the height of one meter (yard.)

TABLE 1:—THE SURFACE TENSION OF VARIOUS SOLUTIONS.

(*Gram-meters per square meter.*)

SOLUTION OF	SP. GR.	*	MEAN.	HIGHEST.	LOWEST.
Salt...............	1.070	6	7.975	8.126	7.796
Kainit.............	1.053	6	7.900	7.993	7.805
Lime..............	1.002	4	7.696	7.750	7.674
Water.............	1.000	18	7.668	7.923	7.506
Acid Phos.........	1.005	4	7.656	7.800	7.563
Plaster........	1.000	9	7.638	7.730	7.572
Soil extract........	1.000	5	7.089	7.166	6.969
Ammonia..........	0.960	6	6.869	6.950	6.826
Urine.............	1.026	10	6.615	6.740	6.471

* Number of measurements from which the mean is taken.

WULLNER GIVES THE FOLLOWING :*

	SP. GR.	TENSION.
Water..............	1.000	7.666
Sulphuric acid.......	1.849	6.333
" "	1.522	7.610
". "	1.127	7.556
Hydrochloric acid....	1.153	7.149
Nitric acid..........	1.500	4.275
" "	1.270	6.768
". "	1.117	7.098
Salt..............	1.200	8.400
Nitrate of potash......	1.137	7.276

*Lehrbuch der Experimental Physik, Vol. I., p. 341.

The soil extract was made by shaking up a little soil with just sufficient water to cover it; the water was afterwards filtered off and used for the determination. It will be seen from the table that this contact with the soil reduced the surface tension of water very considerably. There is little doubt that the surface tension of soil moisture is very low, much lower than that of pure water. Salt and kainit, on the other hand, increase the surface tension of water very considerably and raise it far above that of the soil extract. This probably explains the fact, which has been often commented on, that an application of salt or kainit tends to keep the soil more moist. This has often been remarked in connection with the application to a clover sod. By increasing the surface tension of the soil moisture they increase the power the soil has of drawing water up from below in a dry season.

Ammonia and urine lowered the surface tension of water considerably below that of the soil extract, and far below that of pure water. This, probably, also explains a matter of common observation, that the injudicious use of excessive quantities of organic matter is liable to "burn out" a soil in a dry season, because by reducing the surface tension, water can less readily be drawn up from below.

This opens up a field of investigation on the determination of the surface tension of the moisture in various soils, and a more extensive and more systematic study of the effect of various fertilizing materials on the surface tension of water and soil extract, and it opens up a wide field in its application to practical agriculture and the use of manures and fertilizers.

This effect of fertilizing materials in changing the surface tension of a liquid, and thereby changing the force or power which moves water from place to place in the soil, is only a first effect, as the continued use of these fertilizing materials may change the texture of the soil itself and the relation of the soil to the circulation of water.

II. The Effect of Fertilizers on the Texture of the Soil.

Surface tension may be expressed in another way. The *potential* of a single water particle is the force which would be required to pull it away from the surrounding water particles and remove it beyond their sphere of attraction. For simplicity, it may be described as the total force of attraction between a single particle and all other particles which surround it. With this definition it will be seen that the potential of a particle on an exposed surface of water is only one-half of the potential in the interior of the mass, as half of the particles which formerly surrounded and attracted it were removed when the other exposed surface of water was separated from it. A particle on an exposed surface of water, being under a low potential, will therefore tend to move in towards the center of the mass where the potential, i. e., the total attraction, is greater, and the surface will tend to contract so as to leave the fewest possible number of particles on the surface.

If instead of air there is a solid substance in contact with the water the potential will be greater than on an exposed surface of the liquid, for the much greater number of solid particles will have a greater attraction for the water particle than the air particles had. They may have so great an attraction that the liquid particle on this surface, separating the solid and liquid, may be under greater potential than prevails in the interior of the liquid mass. Then the surface will tend to expand as much as possible for the particles in the interior of the mass of liquid will try to get out onto the surface. This is the reverse of surface tension. It is surface pressure, which may exist on a surface separating a solid and liquid.

If two small grains of clay, suspended in water, come close together, they may be attracted to each other or not, according to the potential of the water particles on the surface of the clay. If the potential of the surface particle of water is less than of a particle in the interior of the mass of liquid, there will be surface tension and the two grains will not come together because this would enlarge the surface area and increase the number of surface particles in the liquid. If, on the other hand, the potential of the particle on the surface of the liquid is greater than the potential of a particle in the interior of the liquid mass, the surface will tend to enlarge and the grains of clay may come close together and be held there with some force, as their close contact increases the number of surface particles in the liquid around them. This probably explains the phenomenon of flocculation, a phenomenon of great importance in agriculture.

Muddy water may remain turbid for an indefinite time. If a trace of lime or salt be added to the water the grains of clay *flocculate*, that is, they come together in loose, light flocks, like curdled milk, and settle quickly to the bottom, leaving the liquid above them clear. Ammonia and some other substances tend to prevent this and to keep the grains apart, or to push them apart if flocculation has already taken place. This is similar to the precipitation of some solid matters from solution. When lime is added to a filtered solution of an extract of stable manure, the organic matter is precipitated in similar loose, bulky masses.

It will be remembered that there is, on an average, about 50 per cent. by volume of empty space in the soil. This empty space is divided up by a vast number of grains of sand and clay. If these grains are evenly distributed throughout the soil, so that the separate spaces between the grains are of nearly uniform size, water will move more slowly through the soil than if the grains of clay, through flocculation, adhered closely together and to the larger grains of sand, making some of the spaces larger and others exceedingly small.

We have, then, this principle to work on in the improvement of soils. In a close, tight clay, through which water moves slowly, the continued use of lime may cause flocculation, the grains of clay may move closer together, leaving larger spaces for the water to move through. On the other hand, there are soils in which the clay is held so closely to the grains of sand as to give the soil all the appearance and properties of a sandy soil, although there is as much clay present as in many a distinctively " clay soil."

Again, in a light sandy land, lime may precipitate the organic matter from solution within the soil, in light, bulky masses, which will fill up the spaces and retard the rate of circulation of water.

And so, if judiciously used, lime may be the " best fertilizer " for a light sandy soil or for a heavy clay land. In the one case, there must be sufficient organic matter for the lime to act on or it will injure the soil; in the other case, there is no such need of organic matter in liming a tight clay soil, and too much of it may be decidedly injurious.

We will speak of this more at length when we come to speak of the application of these principles to the improvement of soils.

III. The Volume of Empty Space in Soils.

There is, on the average, about 50 per cent. by volume of empty space in the soil. The amount in the soil proper will vary with the stage and state of cultivation, but the empty space in the undisturbed subsoil will remain fairly constant. The amount of space has not been determined in the soils of Maryland, for the determination requires that an exact volume of soil be removed from the field, and this takes much time and careful work. This will be made the subject of some future investigation, and for the present our work must be based upon determinations which have been made elsewhere.

The amount of space has been determined in a number of subsoils in South Carolina, in their natural position in the field, taking in a wide range of soil formations. The per cent. by volume of empty space is given in the table following.

TABLE 2:—EMPTY SPACE IN SO. CA. SUBSOILS.

Per Cent. by Volume.

78.	Wedgefield, (sandy land)	41.80
66.	Gourdins	42.82
57.	Sumter	44.10
80.	Lesesne	46.41
57a.	Sumter	47.70
69.	Gourdins, (Mr. Roper)	49.74
64.	Lanes	50.00
74.	Wedgefield, ("Red Hill" formation)	50.03
69a.	Gourdins	50.25
53.	Charlotte, N. C.	52.05
71.	Gourdins, ("Bluff land")	55.40
53a.	Charlotte, N. C.	57.19
76.	Wedgefield, ("gummy land")	58.46
76a.	Wedgefield, ("gummy land")	61.54
42.	Chester, ("pipe clay")	65.12

The first six subsoils, which may be considered essentially sandy, have, on the average, 45.43 per cent. by volume of empty space. The remaining nine subsoils, which are from essentially clay lands, have, on the average, 55.55 per cent. by volume of empty space.

In "How Crops Feed," Johnson gives the weight of a cubic foot of sandy soil as 110 pounds, and of a cubic foot of a clay soil as 75 pounds. This would give about 34 and 55 per cent. by volume of empty space, respectively, in these soils.

It is unfortunate that the term "light soil" has become commonly applied to that which actually weighs a good deal more than an equal bulk of what is called "heavy soil."

In our own work, unless the actual determinations have been made, we have assumed that the subsoil of "light sandy land" has 45 per cent. by volume of empty space, and that of a strong clay land, 55 per cent. If all the space within these soils was filled with water, they would contain 22.41 and 31.55 per cent. *by weight* of water, respectively.

For the empty space in our soil types, to be presently described, we have assigned, as probable, values based on this South Carolina work.

IV. The Relation of Geology to Agriculture.

We shall use in this report certain geological names which may be unfamiliar to many of our readers, and it seems well to insert a section explaining the reason for this and the general relation of geology to agriculture.

We shall show presently that there are well-marked types of soil in this State ; some suited to grass and wheat, others to wheat but rather light for grass, others to tobacco, truck, or left out as barren wastes. The texture and general appearance of these soils differ very much so that one can tell at a glance to what kind of crop each of these types is best adapted. We shall show further, that from this difference in texture, which is so very apparent to the eye, there is a marked difference in the relative rate with which water moves within the soil, and the ease with which the proper amount of water may be maintained and supplied to the crop.

As crops differ in the amount of water which they require, and in the amount of moisture in the soil in which they can best develop, this difference in the relation of these soil types to water probably accounts for the local distribution of plants.

In green-house culture the same kind of soil is used for all kinds of plants, but great judgment is required in watering the plants. Some plants require a very wet soil, others must be kept quite dry. The amount of water required will not be the same at different stages of development of the plant. During the earlier growing period the soil is kept quite wet, but during the fruiting or flowering period the soil is kept much drier. Each class of plants requires in this way special treatment, and it is through this judicious control of the water supply in the soil and the temperature of the air, that the best development of each class of plants is attained.

Our soil types, therefore, in having different relations to the circulation of water, partake somewhat of these artificial conditions in green-house culture, and on each of them certain classes of plants will find conditions of moisture best suited to their growth and development.

Our soils have been formed from the disintegration, or decay, of rocks. The crystalline rocks, such as granite, gabbro and serpentine, from which the soils of Northern Central Maryland are derived, have been formed by the slow cooling of the earth's crust. They are made up of different minerals, the most common of which are quartz, feldspar and mica, cemented together usually with lime or silica. The kind of rock is determined by the kind and relative amount of each of these minerals of which it is made. When the rocks decay, the cementing material is dissolved and carried off, and many of the minerals themselves are changed. Now, the texture or the relative amount of sand and clay contained in the soil resulting from the disintegration of these rocks, will depend upon the kind of rock, that is, upon the minerals of which it was composed.

The material resulting from the disintegration of these rocks is slowly washed away and carried off by streams and rivers. As the current of water becomes slower near the sea, the sand is deposited along a rather narrow shore line, while the finer particles of clay are carried further and deposited over wider areas. The conditions where some parts of this material are being deposited may be favorable to the growth of coral and of various kinds of shell-fish, so that their remains accumulate in beds of great thickness, giving the material for the limestone of the present day. These sediments are thus assorted out by subsidence in water of different velocities, as though they had been sifted and the different grades of material spread out over wide areas.

The sediments, being slowly deposited in beds of great thickness, are converted into rocks through the agency of heat and great pressure to which they are subjected by the accumulation above, and so sandstones, limestones and shales have been formed; the sandstone, where the coarser material has been deposited near the shore; the limestone, where the shells have accumulated; and the shale, where the fine mud has been spread out over a wider area of still water.

It is from the disintegration of these "sedimentary" rocks, as they are called, which have since been raised above the surface of the water, that the soils of Western Maryland have been formed. There are the limestone valleys, where shell-fish were once abundant, and where now is a strong clay soil, well adapted to grass and wheat; the sandstone ridges, some of which, resisting decay, form the mountain ranges, while others, made of finer grains of sand and less firmly cemented together, form some of the fertile hill and valley lands; the shales, in which the grains of mud were so extremely small that they adhere so closely to each other that they do not thoroughly disintegrate, and the soil is filled with fragments of the rock and supports but a scanty mountain pasture.

The soils of Southern Maryland and the Eastern Shore are of more recent origin. The sediments have not, as yet, been subjected to the great heat and pressure required in rock-making, and they are still in the first stages of formation.

Now, geology defines the limits and areas of these different formations and of these different rocks, and, as I have shown, that these rocks determine the texture of the soil, a thorough and detailed geological map of the State should answer for a soil map. Any one familiar with the texture of the soil, or kind of soil, formed by the disintegration of granite, gabbro, and the different kinds of lime. stones, sandstones and shales, should be able to tell by a glance at the map the position and area of each kind of soil. Each color on the map would represent a soil formation of a certain texture, in which the conditions of moisture, under our prevailing climatic conditions, would be best adapted to a certain crop.

Such a geological or soil map would be of the greatest aid to any one interested in the agricultural lands of the State. It seems to me that such a map of the soil formations in this State would be of great benefit to agriculture in the hands of farmers and of those interested in immigration and in the material advancement of the agricultural interests of the State. Not only so, but I think the interest of this work demands the most thorough and detailed geological survey so that each of these soil formations may be carefully located and outlined. The wheat, tobacco, truck and barren lands of Southern

Maryland are each confined to certain different geological formations for their best development, and a geological map of this portion of the State should show the area and distribution of the lands best adapted to these crops.

There is usually some marked and distinctive botanical character in the herbage of these different soil formations. We have pine barrens, white oak lands, black jack lands, chinquapin lands, grass lands, wheat lands and truck lands. These names convey a very good impression of the character and texture of the soil, and they should be more generally used. When a soil formation is spoken of as black jack land, the name conveys a distinct impression of the kind of soil, for a soil must have a certain characteristic texture to produce such a growth.

We have not been able to include this botanical work on the different soil formations of the State this year, but it will be made a subject of careful investigation. In the mean time and until a description better suited to the agricultural interests can be given, the geological names will have to be used to designate these different soil formations.

V. Soil Types.

The soils of the State appear, at first sight, to offer an endless field of research in the great variety often seen on a single farm and in the same field, but a more comprehensive view of the matter will show this to be due to local causes, which have mixed up and modified the original soil formation. These local modifications may be neglected for the present, until the general features of the representative soils of the region have been worked out.

The characteristic properties of great soil formations, or soil types, must first be determined, and then more detailed work may be done in the examination of soils of local interest. Why will not truck, tobacco, wheat and grass grow equally well on all soils? It is not so much a matter of plant food as of the texture of the soil. No addition of mere plant food in the form of fertilizers or manure will change at once a light sandy soil into a good wheat land. It takes no very great experience to tell at a glance the condition of a soil, and to what class of plants it is best adapted. It is from the *appearance* of the soil, that is, from the texture and structure, that this judgment is formed.

This is the key to soil investigations. It is not until this problem has been mastered and these very evident differences in soils have been explained, that the real and full value and application of the chemical determinations in plants and soils will be seen. As a rule, the chemical analysis of a soil will not enable a farmer to determine to what his land is best adapted; but, on the contrary, the farmer, from his experience and judgment, must inform the chemist on this point, and must tell him of the strength and condition of the land.

What are the characteristic properties of a good wheat land, of the best tobacco soil, of the best grass land, of the best land for market truck? What is it in the appearance of a soil which enables a farmer to place it in one or the other of these classes? The truck lands of Southern Maryland are "lighter" in texture than the best tobacco lands, and still "lighter" than the best wheat lands. The wheat lands of Southern Maryland are "lighter" than the grass and wheat lands of Northern and Western Maryland.

It is only after the characteristic properties of a number of soils of well marked agricultural value have been carefully determined that we may hope, by examination and comparison, to suggest methods for the improvement of other soils of local interest. We must have, first of all, a basis of comparison in well known and representative soils.

We have made several extended trips into Southern and Western Maryland, collecting a large number of samples of soils and sub-soils of representative agricultural value and importance. These samples have been arranged in groups, according to their agricultural value and their geological origin; and equal weights of the samples in each group have been mixed together, forming a composite sample representing the *type* of the soil formation. We have, in this way, classified the soils of all the principal agricultural regions of the State, and they are represented by comparatively very few type samples, as shown in the following table:

The formations are not given in the order of their geological origin but according to their agricultural importance and distribution.

TABLE 3 :—SOIL TYPES IN MARYLAND.

SAMPLE.	SOILS ADAPTED TO,	LOCALITIES.	GEOLOGICAL FORMATION.
276.	Pine barrens.	* (2)	Lafayette.
283-4.	Market truck.	(6-8)	Eocene.
285-6.	Tobacco.	(9-9)	Neocene.
279-80.	Wheat.	(7-14)	Neocene.
277-8.	Wheat soil of river terraces.	(5-5)	Columbian terrace.
. . . . .	Barren clay hills.		Potomac.
. . . . .	Grass and wheat.	. . . . .	Trenton chazy limestone.
287-8.	Grass and wheat.	(2-4)	Helderberg limestone.
238.	Grass and wheat.	(1)	Catskill.
281-2.	Grass and wheat.	(4-5)	Triassic red sandstone.
290.	Mountain pasture.	(3)	Oriskany.
289.	Poor mountain pasture.	(6)	Chemung, Hamilton, Niagara, Clinton.

The Lafayette, Eocene, Neocene and Columbian terrace formations occur in Southern Maryland; the Potomac formation is a narrow belt extending across the State on the line of the B. and O. and the B. and P. railroads; the Trenton chazy limestone forms the Frederick and Hagerstown Valleys; the Triassic red sandstone covers a considerable area to the north and south of the Frederick Valley; the Helderberg limestone, Catskill, Oriskany, Chemung, Hamilton, Niagara and Clinton formations form the valleys, hills and mountains of Western Maryland.

In the Piedmont Plateau of Northern Central Maryland, there are grass and wheat soils from gneiss, granite, gabbro and limestone; wheat and tobacco soils from mica schist; corn lands from sandstone; and barren hills from serpentine.

There has been no opportunity this year to collect samples of soils from the Eastern Shore.

There are two or three mountain formations which occur in such small areas that their soils have not been considered here. The coal formation is so uneven, with its succession of sandstones, limestones and shales, which have not been separated on the geological map, that, although it is of importance from covering a large area, it has not, as yet, been considered.

The coarse sands of the quarternary formation, covering the extreme lower part of the State, have not been sampled.

In the table, where a double number is given, the first number refers to the sample of soil, and the second number to the subsoil. Where a single number is given for a type, there is no perceptible difference between the soil and subsoil in the localities visited.

The figures in brackets under * give the number of localities from which samples were taken to make up the samples of type soils and subsoils.

The grass and wheat soils of the different types in the Piedmont Plateau and Western Maryland differ in texture and in relative fertility, and should be distinguished by different botanical characters, but for the present the geological names will be used to designate them.

The truck, limestone and Catskill lands are important soils, which should have more localities represented in the type samples.

To establish a type, samples should be taken from as many localities as possible; from ten localities at least, even in as small a State as Maryland. The type sample is, therefore, a sort of composite sample made by mixing equal weights of samples from a number of localities in each formation.

A description of the samples themselves will be given later. They were taken with a spade, or auger, the *soil* being taken down to the change of color, and the *subsoil* below this to a depth depending upon the nature and depth of the material, usually 12 to 18 inches.

The soil of the pine barrens is a coarse yellow sand, very loose and incoherent when worked, but packed exceedingly hard and tight in the subsoil. The lands are very infertile. These soils should be more carefully examined, and more samples of them should be taken for our type sample, as they cover such an extensive area in Southern Maryland with pine barrens, which will some day, when agricultural lands rise in value, have to be taken up and improved.

Most of the truck supplied to the Baltimore and the larger Northern markets, from this State, is produced on a rather narrow belt bordering the Bay and rivers from Baltimore south to West River. This area is largely in the eocene formation, although far down on the river necks the lands are coarser and belong to a more recent formation.

The truck lands proper are a fine textured, grey or reddish grey, sand. They are naturally fertile, but require care to keep up their fertility. The texture of the soil admits of vast quantities of manure and organic refuse being used for forcing the vegetables, without fear of clogging the soil. The texture of these lands adapt them well to the requirements of market gardening.

The soils are derived from the weathered green sands, similar in composition to the green sand marls of New Jersey, so that in chemical composition they should be rich in potash and phosphoric acid.

The soils are too light in texture for wheat, although, in the high state of cultivation to which they are brought for market truck, good crops of wheat may be produced, but at such a cost, and under such artificial conditions, that the soil cannot, in any sense, be called a wheat soil.

Samples have been taken from too few localities in the truck area to make the type samples of soil and subsoil (Nos. 283-4) perfectly satisfactory. They are probably heavier than the best type of truck land. The collection of these samples has been rather incidental to other work, as most of our attention has been given this year to the tobacco and wheat soils of Southern Maryland. The great truck area between Baltimore and Annapolis is not represented in these samples.

The best tobacco and wheat lands in Southern Maryland, apart from the river terraces, seem to be confined to the diatomaceous earth horizon of the neocene formation, or of a later formation made over out of this same material. The formation extends obliquely across the peninsula, in rather a broad belt from South River and Herring Bay to Pope's Creek on the Potomac River.

The subsoil of the wheat land is a strong clay-loam of a very marked and characteristic texture and yellow color. It is usually not more than 4 to 6 feet deep, resting directly on the white diatomaceous earth, and appears to be formed from this by weathering, as there is no distinct line of separation. The samples of both wheat and tobacco subsoils still contain many diatoms. The weathering of this diatomaceous earth probably takes place quite rapidly on exposure, and some interesting changes occur, including a local accumulation of clay in the yellow subsoil, which should be further studied. We have the material for this work, but it has not been worked out yet.

Wheat and tobacco are commonly grown on the same land in alternate years or in longer rotation, but the strongest and best wheat land is too heavy for tobacco. It gives a large yield but makes a coarse, thick tobacco leaf which is sappy and cures green and does not take on color. The best class of tobacco lands, where the finest grade of tobacco is produced, is of lighter texture and too light for the best wheat production. The best tobacco soils around Upper Marlboro appear to be at a lower elevation than the strongest wheat lands, and are rather heavier in texture than the better grade of tobacco lands in the Nottingham, Aquasco and Chaneyville regions. These latter are more loamy, although they are still over very pure deposits of diatomaceous earth.

At a road cut near Upper Marlboro there is an exposure of diatomaceous earth, probably 30 or 50 feet deep. The upper part of this exposure is very pure white earth, very light and porous. A strong wheat subsoil rests directly on this. The lower part of the exposure is decidedly more sandy in texture, and more like the typical tobacco land. The lighter texture of the tobacco soils may be due to local modifications of original wheat lands, or they may themselves turn into good wheat soils by further weathering, or these tobacco lands may belong to a different horizon of the diatomaceous earth formation. The last seems very probable, but it may be due to different causes in different localities.

Lime is the great fertilizer for all classes of soils in this region. On the lighter soils lime must be used only with organic matter, or it will "burn out the land." Lime every five years, and clover, will keep up their wheat lands. But this rule is being neglected. Lime is applied more rarely and the lands are becoming clover-sick. The wheat and tobacco lands are deteriorating. This cannot be due solely to a loss of plant food from the soil, for there is undoubtedly a change of texture of the soil, very apparent to the eye, which must change the relation of the soil to the circulation of water and to crop production. What these changes are which take place in the soil, must be fully investigated and must be well understood before the most intelligent methods can be proposed for the recovery and improvement of the lands.

The fertile terraces bordering the rivers of Southern Maryland are very level and very uniform in appearance. They extend about half a mile inland from the rivers. The soil is a fine grained loam and the subsoil a yellow clay loam. It would be classed as a good strong wheat soil, very easily worked and naturally very fertile and capable of the highest state of cultivation. They are similar in appearance to the "ridge lands" of the south. Recently the fertile valley lands along the B. & O. R. R., between Baltimore and Washington, (heretofore considered part of the Potomac formation,) as well as other lands in the vicinity of Baltimore, have been classed with the Columbian terrace formation, but these localities are not represented in our type samples.

The barren clay hills crossing the State in a broad belt from Washington, along the two railroads, to the Delaware line, belonging to the Potomac formation, have not been sampled.

The fertile soils of the Frederick and Hagerstown Valleys, formed by the disintegration of the Trenton limestone, are very heavy, red clay, well suited to grass and wheat, They are much stronger than the wheat lands of Southern Maryland. It takes a strong, heavy soil for grass and these are naturally good grass lands. We have a number of samples from different localities but not enough to make a satisfactory type sample.

The Triassic red sandstone covers a considerable area to the north and south of the limestone formation in the Frederick valley, with a dark, indian red, heavy clay soil. It is very productive but is not so safe or certain as the limestone soil. Like the limestone soil, it is greatly benefited by an application of lime.

The Helderberg limestone (cement rock) forms a small area of fertile hill and valley lands west of Hagerstown. The subsoil is a strong yellow clay, naturally well drained, and capable of a high state of cultivation. The land is well adapted to grass and wheat.

The soil appears very uniform in texture and the type sample is considered fairly satisfactory.

The Catskill formation gives a very strong soil, well suited to both grass and wheat. It has a very characteristic dark red color.

The other formations are found in narrow belts forming the hills and mountain ranges, and, so far as I have seen, they are generally very poor and stony. There is often no perceptible difference between the soil and subsoil of these mountain formations, and where they cannot be distinguished, a sample is taken down to 12–18 inches and classed with the subsoils.

A description of the soils and subsoils which have been used to make up the type samples.

PINE BARRENS.

276. Type sample from the following localities:

209. Coarse yellow sand and gravel overlying neocene at Cove Point, three miles north of Drum Point.

210. Coarse yellow sand from bluff at Jones' wharf, Patuxent River.

TRUCK LAND.

283. Type sample of SOIL *from the following localities:*

144. Sandy soil from Patuxent, near Governor's Bridge. Naturally rather poor and unproductive but would make good truck and is typical watermelon land.

167. Sandy soil from a peach orchard at Mitchellville.

170. Soil of light lands west of Hall's Station. From the farm of J. Berry. Very characteristic truck land and of considerable area here.

267. Soil of truck land from farm of J. Birch, South River Neck.

269. Sandy soil of truck land, South River Neck.

271. Soil of truck land east of Hill's Bridge.

284. Type sample of SUBSOIL *from the following localities:*

145. Sandy subsoil from near Governor's Bridge. Under 144.

158. Subsoil of pine land on the "Ridge road" near Cheltenham. A compact red sand which should make good truck land. There is a large area of this land here, probably of Lafayette or possibly of neocene origin.

166. Subsoil from B. D. Mullikin's farm, between Hall's Station and Mitchellville. Characteristic truck land of that region, showing green grains of glauconite and of undoubted eocene origin.

169. Subsoil from peach orchard at Mitchellville, from under 167.

171. Subsoil of light lands west of Hall's Station, under 170.

268. Subsoil truck land, from under 267, from the farm of J. Birch South River Neck.

270. Subsoil of truck land, from under 269, South River Neck.

272. Subsoil truck land, from under 271, east of Hill's Bridge.

These soils and subsoils are undoubtedly of eocene origin except 158, and possibly 269 and 270, which were far down on the Neck and may be of more recent origin.

Tobacco Land.

285. Type sample of soil *from the following localities:*

145. Soil from Chas. W. Sellman's farm near Davidsonville.
Rather light for wheat but makes good tobacco and corn.

161. Loam soil from J. H. Sasscer's farm near Upper Marlboro. A deep loam, lying rather low and much lighter than the best wheat lands. It is a fair type of the tobacco lands of Marlboro district, but is rather heavy for tobacco, making rather a heavy, coarse leaf. It is heavier than the Nottingham or Chaneyville tobacco lands Wheat, on this land, is inclined to go to straw and not produce much grain.

163. Soil of H. H. Sasscer's tobacco land, North Keys. Considered rather heavier than the best type of Nottingham tobacco land. It makes a very fine grade of tobacco.

255. Loam soil from W. H. Hopkins, Bristol. Light in texture and a very fine quality of tobacco land. Considered very fertile but rather light for wheat.

257. Soil of tobacco land from Fred. Sasscer's farm, Upper Marlboro.

259. Soil of tobacco land from the river terrace at Nottingham. The soil is coarser than most of the river terraces examined. This grade of soil appears to be of rather small area. The terraces extend about half a mile inland from the river and produce a fine quality of tobacco.

261. Soil from a farm near Chaneyville. It is considered the very finest grade of tobacco land.

263. Soil of a fine grade of tobacco land near Nottingham.

265. Soil of a very fine type of tobacco land from the farm of J. F. Talbott, Chaneyville.

286. Type sample of subsoil *from the following localities:*
Samples 148, 162, 164, 256, 258, 260, 262, 264, 266, from under the soils just given, and in the corresponding order.

These soils and subsoils are of neocene origin or formed of neocene material, except 259, 260, 263, 264. Diatoms were found in most of the subsoils. The finest tobacco lands are lighter in texture than the best wheat lands.

WHEAT LAND.

279. Type sample of SOIL *from the following localities:*

140. Loam soil from near Davidsonville, fairly representing the wheat lands of this locality. It appears somewhat light for wheat, and is not considered as productive as it was years ago. It does not produce the clover crops it once did, which were such an excellent preparation for wheat. The lands have deteriorated. The finest wheat lands now are the hill lands where this loam has not accumulated, or has been removed by subsequent washing, leaving exposed a yellow clay loam like 142.

154. Clay soil from J. H. Sasscer's farm near Upper Marlboro. Very fine wheat land, similar to the Davidsonville and West River lands. Too heavy for tobacco, the plant being sappy and curing green. These lands are of considerable area around Marlboro, extending up nearly to Mitchellville on the east of the railroad, and forming the bottom lands and hills, west of the Western Branch of the Patuxent, but becoming much lighter in texture south of Marlboro.

178. Clay soil at the base of the neocene, at Herring Bay. Good strong wheat land, very similar to the preceding localities.

183. Soil of wheat land from James Chapman, Pope's Creek. This land carries a good grass sod.

249. Soil of wheat land from J. F. Talbott, Chaneyville.

251. Soil of the fertile wheat lands of West River.

253. Loam soil from Mt. Zion. Very characteristic wheat land, similar to those of Davidsonville and West River.

280. Type sample of SUBSOIL *from the following localities:*

141. Loam subsoil from under 140, from near Davidsonville. It has good body but not the consistancy of the next sample. It fairly represents the lands around here where washing has not occurred. The loam is from two to four feet deep.

142. Yellow clay subsoil from under the above, taken in a road cut. This forms the very best wheat land when exposed. It has the very characteristic color and texture of the best wheat lands in Southern Maryland.

155. Clay subsoil of wheat land from under 154, from the farm of J. H. Sasscer, near Upper Marlboro.

156. Yellow clay subsoil under the "gravelly lands" of Rosaryville. This is undoubtedly neocene or neocene material. A fair quality of diatomaceous earth was found in a road cut near by, directly underlying this and gradually passing from the white earth into the yellow clay above. The country is covered generally with a thin layer of fine gravel, which is hardly noticed in cultivated fields and is often absent. The gravel extends down into the undisturbed clay and is probably part of the same formation, although there may be a light coating of Lafayette here, made out of the neocene material. The lands make a very fine quality of tobacco but are generally too light for wheat. When this clay is exposed without the gravel, however, it makes a very fine wheat land. On Mr. Holloway's place, between Rosaryville and Woodyard, and near where this sample was taken, they made a very fair quality of brick some years ago from the subsoil of the wheat field.

179. Clay subsoil of the wheat lands of Herring Bay, from under 178.

180. Yellow clay subsoil from over diatomaceous earth, from a bluff three miles north of Plum point.

184. Yellow clay subsoil of wheat land, from under 183, from the farm of James Chapman, Pope's Creek.

245. Subsoil f wheat land opposite the church at Davidsonville. It is in a fine state of cultivation.

246. Subsoil of wheat land about one half mile west of Davidsonville.

247. Subsoil of wheat land, now in grass, from the farm of James Iglehart, Davidsonville.

248. Subsoil of wheat land from the farm of P. H. Israel, Davidsonville.

250. Subsoil of wheat land from the farm of J. F. Talbott, Chaneyville. From under 249.

252. Subsoil of wheat land, from under 251, South River.

254. Subsoil of wheat land, from under 253, Mt. Zion.

River Terrace.

277. *Type sample of* soil *from the following localities:*

198. Loam soil from a wheat field opposite Benedict.

200. Loam soil from a corn field below St. Mary's. This soil is naturally fertile and is capable of great improvement. An excellent wheat soil.

202. Loam soil from Mr. Broome's wheat land, St. Mary's.

204. Loam soil from a wheat field opposite St. Mary's.

206. Loam soil from Clifton Beach. Good wheat land.

278. *Type sample of* subsoil *from the following localities:* Samples 199, 201, 203, 205, 207, are subsoils from under the above soils, given in the same order.

HELDERBERG LIMESTONE.

287. *Type sample of* soil *from the following localities:*

221. Soil from near Hancock. Very fertile grass and wheat land.

222. Soil from near Hancock.

288. *Type sample of* subsoil *from the following localities:*

220. Very fertile grass and wheat land two miles west of Hancock. No change in 18 inches.

223. Subsoil near Hancock.

224. Characteristic yellow subsoil of the Helderberg limestone, from a wheat field two miles west of Hancock. Contains many small fragments of undecomposed rock.

225. Subsoil from near Cumberland. Naturally rather poor but has good body and is very fertile where improved.

CATSKILL.

238. Type sample of the Catskill formation, from near Mt. Savage. Good strong land for grass and wheat. Has a characteristic, dark red color.

ORISKANY.

290. *Type sample of Oriskany from the following localities:*

226 and 227, from near Cumberland, and 228, from Hancock. The formation is not very uniform in texture. The localities visited have rather a fine textured soil, naturally poor but capable of some improvement. The formation occurs only in narrow belts capping hills and mountains, and is not of much extent in the State.

CHEMUNG, HAMILTON, NIAGARA AND CLINTON.

289. Type sample from the following localities:

234. Subsoil of the Hamilton shale, from near Mt. Savage. Naturally very poor but capable of some improvement as it has good body.

235. Hamilton shale, from Cumberland. Poor lands—mostly thin mountain pastures.

236 and 237, Chemung from two localities near Mt. Savage. Naturally rather poor land.

239. Niagara from near Cumberland. Poor but has good body and is capable of some improvement.

240. Clinton shale from near Cumberland. Lands naturally poor but have good body.

These formations appear so much alike in texture and agricultural features that they are all included in the one type. They are nearly all hill and mountain pastures, naturally poor and not capable of great improvement, except as garden spots and at great expense. The soil or rather subsoil, for there is little or no difference, is a very fine grained, powdery material, filled with small fragments of the original rock.

VI. MECHANICAL ANALYSIS OF THE TYPE SOILS.

The soils of these type formations differ so much in texture that the difference is quite apparent to the eye. Some are coarser than others, the grains are larger and there are fewer of them in a given weight of soil. The first thing done, in the examination of the soil, was to make a mechanical analysis by separating the grains into groups, according to size. The approximate number of grains in each group was then calculated and this shows how much the empty space in the soil has been divided up and, relatively, how fast water will move through the different soils.

For the greatest accuracy, the grains should be separated into a large number of groups, so that all the grains in each group shall be very nearly of the same size, but the analysis takes so long that we have used only eight groups. The separations were made substantially after Johnson and Osborn's "beaker method." We have taken .0001 mm. as the lowest limit of size of the grains of clay, based on many measurements we have made. The clay group has relatively wide limits (.005–.0001 mm.) but we have not attempted a further separation than this. A millimeter (1 mm.) is equivalent to about 1-25th of an inch, so that the smallest grains of clay are about 1-25400 inch or .0000039 inch in diameter.

Table 4, gives the results of the mechanical analysis of the type samples of the subsoils of the five formations in Southern Maryland. The analyses and calculations based on the other type samples will not be completed in time for this report.* The subsoils have been taken up first, as the texture of the subsoil is more important in determining the nature of the land and its relation to the water supply of crops than that of the soil itself.

TABLE 4:—MECHANICAL ANALYSES OF TYPE SUBSOILS.

Diameter. mm.	Conventional names.	276. Pine barrens.	284. Truck.	286. Tobacco.	280. Wheat.	278. River terrace.
2–1	Gravel	†4.87	0.68	1.36	0.00	1.60
1–.5	Coarse sand	9.15	2.89	2.13	0.42	1.51
.5–.25	Medium sand	38.37	21.85	7.78	1.81	4.15
.25–.1	Fine sand	33.28	25.82	16.57	8.59	4.84
.1–.05	Very fine sand	3.52	18.38	19.83	32.06	8.54
.05–.01	Silt.	3.47	9.48	25.41	23.65	44.92
.01–.005	Fine silt	1.55	3.37	4.52	6.77	5.78
.005–.0001	Clay	3.75	15.30	17.95	22.55	25.85
		97.96	97.77	95.55	95.85	97.19
Organic matter, water, loss..		2.04	2.23	4.45	4.15	2.81

† This includes 1.81 per cent. larger than 2mm. in diameter.

NOTE.—Each of these type samples is made up of samples from a number of localities in each soil formation.

The results in this table are confusing from the mass of figures, and from the fact that each group has to be given a special value, depending upon the size of the soil grains which it contains; a per cent. of clay having far more value than an equal amount of gravel. From this table alone it would be difficult to judge of the texture of the soils.

VII. APPROXIMATE NUMBER OF GRAINS PER GRAM OF SOIL.

From the results in Table 4 we have calculated the approximate number of grains of sand and clay in one gram of the subsoils, as

*This matter has since been completed and will be given in an appendix.

given in Table 5. These figures are, of course, only approximate and the numbers are far beyond our comprehension. They may be used relatively, however, in comparing one soil with another.

TABLE 5:—APPROXIMATE NUMBER OF GRAINS PER GRAM OF SUBSOIL.*

Diameter. mm.	Conventional names.	276. Pine barrens.	284. Truck.	286. Tobacco.	280. Wheat.	278. River terrace.
2–1	Gravel	7	1	3	0	3
1–.5	Coarse sand	160	50	38	7	26
.5–.25	Medium sand	5 356	3 056	1 114	258	583
.25–.1	Fine sand	45 700	35 530	23 320	12 050	6 701
.1–.05	Very fine sand	61 380	321 200	354 500	571 200	150 200
.05–.01	Silt	945 900	2 589 000	7 101 000	6 588 000	12 340 000
.01–.005	Fine Silt	27 030 000	58 880 000	80 790 000	120 700 000	101 600 000
.005–.0001	Clay	1 664 000 000	6 806 000 000	8 170 000 000	10 230 000 000	11 570 000 000
		1 692 088 503	6 867 828 837	8 258 269 975	10 357 871 515	11 084 097 513

*There are about 453 grams in one pound.

It will be remembered that the texture of the soil is determined by the size and, therefore, by the number of grains per unit weight or volume of soil. In this table it will be seen that the number of grains in the fine "silt" and "clay" groups so far exceed the number in all the other groups combined, that they, and especially the clay, actually determine the extent of subdivision of the empty space in the soil. The other groups may be neglected, for practically, the effect of the gravel and sand, is only to diminish the amount of clay per unit weight or volume of soil. The amount of clay is, therefore, a very important factor in any soil as it practically determines the subdivision of the empty space and the texture of the land.

TABLE 6:—TOTAL NUMBER OF GRAINS IN ONE GRAM.

(*Summary of Results in Table 5.*)

276......	Pine barrens...........	*(2)	1 692 000 000
284......	Truck....................	(8)	6 868 000 000
286......	Tobacco............ ..	(9)	8 258 000 000
280......	Wheat	(14)	10 358 000 000
278......	River terrace.....	(5)	11 684 000 000
....	Limestone (grass land)...	(1)	24 653 000 000

* Number of localities represented.

The summary of the results in Table 6 places the soils at once in their true agricultural relation. It suggests also a method for the classification of soils.

From the mechanical analysis of the samples which were used to make up these type samples, and perhaps of a large number of other soils of known agricultural value, it should be possible to determine the smallest and the largest number of grains per gram of soil where these different crops could be successfully grown. For example, no crop can be successfully grown, except under highly artificial conditions of manuring with organic matter, or by irrigation, on a soil having so few as *one thousand seven hundred million* grains per gram. Good market truck is grown on a soil having *six thousand eight hundred million* grains. Now what is the limit between these two figures where the soil becomes too light for market truck? Good wheat is grown on a soil having *ten thousand million* grains per gram, and this must be near the limit of profitable wheat production, for *eight thousand million* grains per gram gives a soil rather too light for wheat, but well suited to tobacco. A soil having *ten thousand million* grains per gram is too light for grass, which thrives on a limestone soil having *twenty-four thousand million*. Our type soils should, therefore, show the range for the profitable production of a given crop. We should be able also from the mechanical analysis of an unknown soil to give it its true agricultural place by reference to these established soil types.

It is not to be inferred from these statements that wheat cannot be grown on a soil having so few as *one thousand million* grains per gram. This number represents merely the skeleton, or framework, of the soil. As we shall see later, this may be so filled in and modified by organic matter as to enable it to support a good wheat crop, but at such an expense as to put it far outside the limit of profitable culture. This is a matter of judgment and experience. The soil types give only the skeleton structure of the soil.

Nor is it to be inferred that wheat may be grown on all soils having *ten thousand million* grains or more per gram with equal success, for the relation of these soils to water, upon which the cropping depends, is a matter not only of how much the space within the soil is subdivided, that is, how many grains there are, but depends also upon the way these grains are arranged. We will develop this idea further, when we come to speak of the cause of the deterioration of lands and of their improvement.

VII. Approximate Extent of Surface Area per Cubic Foot of Soil.

We are able, from the foregoing results, based on the mechanical anlysis of the soils, to calculate the approximate extent of surface area of the grains of clay and sand in a given weight or volume of soil.

A solid block of granite, one foot square and one foot high, would have six square feet of surface area, but when this cube of solid rock disintegrates, forming or leaving a cubic foot of soil, half of the rock is dissolved and carried off and what remains is split up into a vast number of separate grains of sand and clay. If a soil were made up of fragments as large as this cubic foot of rock, then, even if the proper water supply could be maintained in the soil, it would be impossible for our staple crops to get their needed food supply. The soil moisture and the roots themselves can only dissolve food material from the surface of the rock. The rock is exceedingly insoluble and the amount of plant food which could be dissolved and extracted from six square feet of surface by water or roots, would be exceedingly small and entirely insufficient for the needs of any of our staple crops.

The soil, however, resulting from the disintegration of such a rock has an enormous extent of surface area if all the surface on the separate grains of sand and clay be considered. Table 7 gives the approximate extent, in square centimeters, of the surface area in one gram of our type subsoils and of a limestone subsoil from Frederick Valley. Table 8 shows the approximate number of *square feet* of surface area in *one cubic foot* of soil.

TABLE 7:—SURFACE AREA (*sq. cm.*) PER GRAM OF SUBSOIL.

Diameter. mm.	Conventional names.	276. Pine barrens.	284. Truck.	286. Tobacco.	280. Wheat.	279. River terrace.	Limestone.
2–1	Gravel	0.5	0.1	0.2	0.0	0.2	0.0
1–.5.	Coarse sand	2.8	1.0	0.7	0.1	0.5	0.0
.5–.25	Medium sand	23.6	13.5	4.9	1.1	2.6	0.1
.25–.1	Fine sand	43.9	34.1	22.4	11.6	6.4	0.4
.1–.05	Very fine sand	10.8	56.7	62.5	100.9	26.5	7.6
.05–.01	Silt	26.7	73.1	200.7	186.2	348.7	221.3
.01–.005	Fine silt	47.7	104.1	142.8	213.2	179.5	344.3
.005–.0001	Clay	339.8	1387.0	1668.0	2089.0	2360.0	5000.0
		495.8	1669.6	2102.2	2602.1	2924.4	5573.7

TABLE 8:—SQUARE FEET OF SURFACE PER CUBIC FOOT OF SUBSOIL.

276	Pine barrens....	23 940 square feet.
284......	Truck..........	74 130 " "
286......	Tobacco.	84 850 " "
280	Wheat..........	94 540 " "
278......	River terrace....	106 200 " "
		(2.3 acres.)
	Limestone.......	~~202 600~~ square feet.
		(158 000 ~~acres~~.)

It will be seen that there are upwards of 24,000 square feet of surface area in a cubic foot of the subsoil of the pine barrens, no less than 100,000 square feet, or 2.3 acres, of surface area in a cubic foot of the subsoil of the river terrace, and 158,000 square feet of surface area in a cubic foot of the limestone subsoil.

These figures seem vast, but they are probably below, rather than above, the true values on account of the wide range of the diameters of the clay group, as given in the table. This gives an enormous area for the roots and soil moisture to act on for the extraction of plant food from the mineral elements of the soil. Instead of the few square feet offered by the cube of granite, there are now several acres of surface area, for the roots to range over, in search of food and for the water to act on, in a single cubic foot of soil. This great extent of surface and of surface attraction, which has been described as potential in Section II., gives the soil great power to absorb moisture from the air, and to absorb and hold back mineral matters from solution. A smooth surface of glass will attract and hold, by this surface attraction, an appreciable amount of moisture from the surrounding air. A cubic foot of soil, having 100,000 square feet of surface, should be able to attract and hold a considerable amount of moisture from the air.

When a soil is only slightly moistened with water there will be nearly as much exposed water-surface as the surface of the soil grains themselves. The amount of energy or tension on such an extent of water-surface will be very great and it is this which enables a soil to draw up the large amount of water needed by the crop.

In all of these relations, the extent of surface gives the soil a certain strength and value which must have an important bearing on crop production and distribution.

IX. The Circulation of Water in these Type Soils.

We have shown that the number of grains per gram, places these type soils in their true agricultural relation. We have now to show the reason for this in the difference in their relation to the circulation of water, and the ease with which a definite quantity of water can be supplied to a given crop.

We will assume that the grains in all the soils have the same mean arrangement, then the relative rate of circulation, other things being equal, will depend upon how much space there is in the soil and upon how much this space is subdivided.

For the reasons which have already been given, we have not been able to determine the amount of space in the soils which were used to make up the type samples. The determinations require much time and great care to remove a definite volume of soil from the field, and this must be made the subject of some future investigation. From our work in South Carolina on similar soils, which has been referred to, we have assumed the per cent. of empty space in each of the soil types, given in the following tables. These values, therefore, are not exact determinations, but are thought to be approximately correct. It is important to observe that the coarser soils have less space and, consequently, when this space is completely filled with water, the sandy soils will contain less water than the clay soils. In a cubic foot of the sandy soils there is considerably less than half a cubic foot of empty space; in the same volume of the clay soils there is *over* half a cubic foot of space for water to move in. This difference in the amount of space in the different soils, gives rise to an important modification of the relative rate of circulation, when the soils are saturated, and when they are short of saturation.

The empty space in agricultural soils is hardly ever completely filled with water. The most favorable amount of water in the soil, for growing plants, as Hellriegel and others have shown, is from 30 to 50 per cent. of the water-holding capacity of the soil. As a light sandy land has less space and will hold less water than a clay soil, the most favorable amount of water for vegetation will be less than in a clay soil. We have repeatedly found in actual determinations, less water in light lands than in heavy clay soils, and it is a matter of observation and experience that light lands are drier than heavy clay soils.

The reason for this follows from the fact that water circulates more freely in these light soils, by reason of the fewer grains and the less amount of subdivision of the empty space, and after a moderate rain the water passes down more readily into the lower depths of the subsoil.

After the excess of rainfall has passed down through the soils and, equilibrium is established, there will be less water in the light lands than in the clay soils. If, then, a definite quantity of water is required, by the crop in a given time, it can move up to the plant through the sandy soil more readily, but there is less *water-surface* in the light land to contract, that is, there is less force to pull the water up.   These points are well brought out in the following calculations of the relative rate of circulation of water in these type subsoils.

If we assume in the first place, that all the soils contain the same amount of water, namely 12 per cent. (the most favorable amount in the wheat land,) the relative rate of circulation will be as follows:

No.	Soil.	Space.	Water-content.	Relative time.
276....	Pine barrens....	40 per cent.	12 per cent.	17
284....	Truck..........	45 " "	12 " "	43
286....	Tobacco........	50 " "	12 " "	68
280 ...	Wheat..........	55 " "	12 " "	92
278....	River terrace....	55 " "	12 " "	100

If it takes 100 minutes for a quantity of water to pass down through a certain depth of the subsoil of the river terrace, the same weight of water could pass down through the subsoil of the truck land in 43 minutes, and through the subsoil of the pine barrens in 17 minutes.   It could not move up so readily for there is less *water surface*, as we have shown, to contract and pull it up from below.

When equilibrium is established and the water is moving down with about the *same rate* in each of the subsoils, there will be about 6.5 per cent. in the subsoil of the pine barrens, 9 per cent. in the truck land and 12 per cent. in the subsoil of the river terrace, as follows:

No.	Soil.	Space.	Water-content.	Relative time.
276....	Pine barrens....	40 per cent.	6.6 per cent.	102
284....	Truck	45 " "	9.0 " "	102
286....	Tobacco........	50 " "	10.5 " "	102
280....	Wheat.	55 " "	11.7 " "	101
278....	River terrace...	55 " "	12.0 " "	100

This would be about the relative amount of water found in these subsoils some time after rain.   When the subsoil of the river terrace contains 12 per cent. of water, that of the pine barren would contain about 6.5 per cent., that of the truck land, 9 per cent.

The interesting question suggested above, comes up here again.   If the rate of circulation of water through the light truck land with 9 per cent. of water present in the subsoil, is the same as in the wheat soil of the river terrace with 12 per cent. of water, (the most favorable amount for wheat), then why are not the light truck lands as good for wheat as the other? And the explanation given above is only made clearer through these tables, that while gravity acts with a constant force, *with* surface tension, to pull the water down, surface tension alone has to pull the water up to the crop *against gravity;* and there is less surface tension, less contracting power, less force, to pull up a given weight of water in a given time in the light land than in the other. The wheat crop would suffer on such a soil in a warm, dry spell, when it had to depend on water being supplied it from below.

We have shown that there is less space in the light truck land than in the wheat soils, but the soil grains being larger, there are fewer of them, and the space is not divided up so much. Each separate space is larger and, when the soil is short of saturation, the water moves faster.

If however the soils are fully saturated, the volume of empty space has an important value in retarding the rate of movement. There is less volume of space in the light lands, less water can be crowded into it than in the wheat soils, and so, when the spaces in the soils are fully saturated, the rate of movement will be relatively slower than in the wheat soils.

The relative rate of movement of water through these different subsoils when all the space is filled with water, will be as follows:

No.	Soil.	Space.		Water-content.			Relative time.
276..	Pine barrens..	40 per cent.		20.10 per cent. (Sat.)			63
284..	Truck	45 " "		22.41 ' " "			120
286..	Tobacco	50 " "		27.42 " " "			103
280..	Wheat	55 " "		31.55 " " "			92
278..	River terrace.	55 " "		31.55 " " "			100

If all the space is filled with water, as assumed in Table 9, the subsoils will contain, respectively, 25, 28, 31, 33, and 33 pounds of water per cubic foot. If a given quantity of water passes down through a depth of saturated subsoil of the river terrace in 100 minutes, it would take about 120 minutes for the same quantity of water to go down through the same depth of the saturated subsoil of the light truck land. This probably explains a matter of common observation and experience, that crops on light sandy lands are more injured in excessive wet seasons than crops on heavier soils. The excess of water cannot be removed so fast by the light lands, when saturated, as in the heavier soils.

There are other interesting lines of thought, and explanations of other matters of common observation and experience, suggested by this line of reasoning, which may be followed out at another time as the limits of this report allow of only a concise narrative account of the work and a very general statement of the application of the results.

X. The Improvement of Soils.

When we consider that desserts are barren only from the lack of water and that where water is supplied they become fertile and productive as other lands; and when we consider the immense crops raised in dry and arid countries by irrigation as well as the difference in the yield of crops in our own state, in wet and in dry seasons, and other evidences which will be published at another time, we are forced to the conclusion that vegetation is very largely dependent for its developement and growth upon a proper water supply, and that the whole art of cultivation and manuring is based upon the possible control of the water supply within the soil.

We have shown the principles upon which this control is based; we come now to an application of these principles to the improvement of soils.

The agricultural lands of this state have generally good surface drainage. They have a small quantity of organic matter which is fairly uniform in amount in the soils of the different soil formations. If such a soil is shown by a mechanical analysis to have not less than *ten thousand million* grains per gram, it has the structure, or frame work, for a good wheat soil and should be classed as such. If it does not produce good wheat crops, or if it has deteriorated from a more fertile condition, there may be some change in the structure of the soil through a change in the arrangement of the soil grains.

The case must be studied as a physician considers the condition of a sick person; a diagnosis must be made to determine the cause of the trouble. The symptoms both of the soil and of the crops must be carefully studied. If the soil is rather close and too retentive of moisture, the plants are large and sappy and give a small yield of fruit or seed in proportion to the size of the plant and the amount of food material gathered by the plant from the atmosphere and soil. The crop is also inclined to be late it maturing.

If the soil is dry and leachy, the plants are small and give a small yield, but the yield is relatively larger in proportion to the food material that has been stored up.

Other symptoms, besides this relation of the yield of grain and fruit to the size of the plant, that is, to the amount of food material stored up by the plant, offer evidence as to the condition of the soil and the changes needed for its improvement, such as the vigor of the plant, the way it develops and grows, the diseases and insect ravages to which it is subject, and the influence of wet and dry seasons on the crop production.

The cotton crop at the South is very sensitive to these conditions of environments. The wheat crop more readily adapts itself to the conditions under which it is grown, and is, therefore, not so sensitive or reliable for showing up these soil conditions.

There is need of an instrument, or a method, to show the actual rate with which water moves both up and down within the soil in its natural position in the field, and such a method must be devised, for the information is of great importance.

It has been shown how the relative rate of circulation of water may be calculated from the mechanical analysis of the soil. If this calculated rate could be compared with the actual rate of circulation in the soil in the field, it would indicate the relative arrangement of the soil grains, so that if we had such a method there would be no such necessity for studying the symptoms of the plant to tell in what direction, and how far, the conditions in a soil have departed from the typical conditions required by a given crop, or natural to the soil formation.

If the rate of circulation of water within the soil is shown, by actual observation or by its effect upon plants, to be slower than the rate calculated from the mechanical analysis, and slower than the rate of circulation in the typical soil for that crop, the texture of the soil may be changed by changing the arrangement of the soil grains. The smallest grains may be drawn closer to the larger ones, making some of the spaces larger and others exceedingly small. Lime, kainite and phosphoric acid seem to have this effect, as their continued use makes the soil more loamy, looser in texture, and less retentive of moisture.

Many of our agricultural lands need improvement in the other direction, they need to be made closer in texture and more retentive of moisture. We have found that ammonia, the caustic alkalies, carbonate of soda, and probably many other substances, possibly organic substances in general, tend to prevent this flocculation and to push the smaller grains further apart, making the spaces within the soil of a more uniform size and thus retarding the rate of circulation of the soil moisture. We cannot say what practical value this will have in its application to agriculture until more work has been done.

When a solution of organic matter comes in contract with lime, kainite, acid phosphate, and with certain soils, the organic matter is precipitated from solution in light, bulky masses, and these masses may fill up the spaces within the soil with solid matter which not only retards the rate of circulation of water downward by gravity, but, by increasing the extent of water-surface within the soil, it also assists in pulling water up from below.

If so much organic matter is added to the soil that it cannot be curdled or precipitated from solution, it may be injurious in the soil by reducing the surface tension of the soil moisture, the force which draws the water to the plant as needed. The judicious use of lime, kainite or acid phosphate, along with the organic matter, will insure the precipitation of the organic-matter from solution and thus give a value to the application which it would not otherwise have had.

This gives a value to stable manure, out of all proportion to the amount of plant food which it contains. Lime, also, either alone or when acting with organic matter, has a distinct value for all classes of land. The nitrogenous matters in the stable manure, and in other organic matters, would determine the value as a fertilizer, for it is only the nitrogenous compounds which are so easily precipitated from solution by the mineral matters of the soil and of fertilizers. If the carbohydrates, such as starch, sugar and woody fibre, could be as readily precipitated from solution in light, bulky masses, by lime and the mineral matters of the soil, then sawdust or other organic refuse containing little nitrogen, would have nearly the same fertilizing value as the more expensive nitrogenous materials.

The whole history of plat experiments shows that it is not the plant which is to be manured for, but the soil conditions must be changed to produce the plant.

The corn plant on one soil requires potash, on another soil, phosphoric acid, on another soil, nitrogen, and again on another soil a combination of two or more of these fertilizers. On the whole, there is no such fertilizer in our State for wheat as lime, used alone or acting with organic matter.

Plat experiments frequently give a larger yield when lime, salt or plaster is used, and even when nothing at all has been added to the soil, than when the more expensive plant foods have been used. Especially when acid phosphate or potash has been used alone, the yield is often smaller than where nothing has been added to the soil.

Under ordinary conditions, our crops do not require special plant foods, but they all have somewhat different habits of growth and development and can best gather food under somewhat different physical conditions. We have seen how these different fertilizing materials change the physical conditions in the soil.

This opens up a new and wide field for investigation in the study of the physical conditions of the soil in their relation to plant growth and developement, and the effect thereon of the different fertilizers and manures. It will be through this study that the true theory of fertilization will be seen, and an interpretation and added value be given to the immense amount of chemical data, which has accumulated, relating to the soil.

Correction :—Through an oversight, part of the explanation of the phenomenon of flocculation on page 258 was transposed. It should read as follows : If the potential of the surface particle of water is less than of a particle in the interior of the mass of liquid, there will be surface tension, and the two grains will come together and be held with some force, as their close contact will diminish the number of surface particles in the liquid. If, on the other hand, the potential of the particle on the surface of the liquid is greater than the potential of a particle in the interior of the liquid mass, the surface will tend to enlarge, and the grains of clay will not come close together, as their close contact will diminish the number of surface particles in the liquid around them.

M. W.

APPENDIX.

Since the main part of my report was written, I have been able to secure the services of Mr. F. P. Veitch and Mr. J. B. Latimer, graduates of the class of 1891 of the Agricultural College. Mr. Veitch has completed the mechanical analysis of our type subsoils, which enables me to present the results here, with a short discussion.

The mechanical analysis of these type subsoils, given in Table 13, is based upon the "fine earth," or material smaller than 2 *mm.* in

TABLE 10:—MECHANICAL ANALYSIS OF TYPE SUBSOILS.

Diameter. mm.	Conventional names.	276. Pine barrens.	284. Truck.	286. Tobacco.	290. Oriskany.	280. Wheat.	278. River terrace.	282. Triassic.	238. Catskill.	289. Shales.	288. Helderberg limestone.
2–1	Gravel	*4.87	0.68	1.36	0.64	0.0	1.60	0.00	0.00	0.05	†1.34
1–.5	Coarse sand	9.15	2.89	2.13	0.81	0.42	1.51	0.23	0.11	0.16	0.33
.5–.25	Medium sand	38.37	21.85	7.78	3.50	1.81	4.15	1.29	0.42	0.80	1.08
.25–.1	Fine sand	33.28	25.82	16.57	23.97	8.59	4.84	4.03	2.63	2.01	1.02
.1–.05	Very fine sand	3.52	18.38	19.83	34.76	32.06	8.54	11.57	11.35	6.70	6.94
.05–.01	Silt	3.47	9.48	25.41	10.03	23.65	44.92	38.97	40.23	31.63	29.05
.01–.005	Fine Silt	1.55	3.37	4.52	3.03	6.77	5.78	8.84	10.90	14.21	11.03
.005–.0001	Clay	3.75	15.30	17.95	20.30	22.85	25.85	32.70	33.32	39.36	43.44
		97.96	97.77	95.55	97.04	95.85	97.19	97.63	98.96	94.91	94.23
Organic matter, water, loss :		2.04	2.23	4.45	2.96	4.15	2.81	2.37	1.04	5.09	5.77

*This includes 1.81 per cent. coarser than 2 mm.

†This includes 0.82 per cent. coarser than 2 mm,

diameter. Three of these subsoils were not thoroughly disintegrated, but contained small fragments of rock, which were separated out and weighed, the remaining fine earth being used for the mechanical analysis. The samples contained the following per cent. of coarse and of fine material.

	290	238	289
	Oriskany.	Catskill.	Shales.
Coarser than 2 *mm.*	5.80	21.28	17.23
" Fine earth "	94.20	78.72	82.77

We have not, as yet, attempted to study the effect of these fragments of rock upon the relation of the soils to the movement of water, but have confined ourselves to the simpler study of soils having no coarse fragments, and we will, therefore, disregard this coarse material for the present, and treat the soils as though composed only of the fine earth. It may well be, that in some localities disintegration has gone further than where these samples were taken, and that these same soil formations there contain no coarse fragments of the undecomposed rock. Our results should apply directly to such a soil.

TABLE 11:—APPROXIMATE NUMBER OF GRAINS IN ONE GRAM OF SUBSOIL.

276.	Pine barrens.	1 692 000 000
284.	Truck.	6 868 000 000
286.	Tobacco.	8 258 000 000
290.	Oriskany.	9 154 000 000
280.	Wheat.	10 358 000 000
278.	River terrace.	11 684 000 000
282.	Triassic red sandstone.	14 736 000 000
238.	Catskill.	14 839 000 000
289.	Shales (Hamilton, &c.)	18 295 000 000
288.	Helderberg limestone.	19 638 000 000
. . . .	Trenton chazy limestone.	24 653 000 000

Table 11 gives the approximate number of grains of sand and clay in one gram of these type subsoils, and the results confirm what has been stated before, that the soils thus arranged are in the order of their relative agricultural value.

The Oriskany formation is of very small agricultural importance, as it has such a small area in the State, occurring in narrow belts, the widest being hardly more than a mile across. It has a place in the table between the tobacco and wheat soils of Southern Maryland.

The Triassic red sandstone and the Catskill formations are shown to have about the same structure. The soils themselves are very similar, and, except for their distinct geological and geographical positions, they should be grouped as a single soil type. The Catskill formation covers a considerable area in the valley between Sideling Hill and Town Hill Mountains, and again between the Great Savage Mountain and the Meadow Mountain, with a very narrow belt near Dan's Mountain, between Mt. Savage and Cumberland, where our single sample of the formation was obtained. This is an important soil formation, which should be more carefully studied, and of which more samples should be taken. From the general appearance of the land, as seen from the train in passing, there does not seem to be as much undecomposed rock in the soils of these wider areas as is contained in the sample, which is given here. I should estimate that there are about 320 square miles of this Catskill formation in Western Maryland, and about the same area of the Triassic red sandstone to the north and south of the Frederick Valley.

The Hamilton and Chemung shales have their widest exposure around Hancock and on either side of the Polish Mountain, covering perhaps 125 square miles. The Clinton and Niagara shales occur in very narrow ridges, giving a much smaller exposure than this. The mechanical analysis of the type sample of these formations gives 39.36 per cent. of "clay," or, approximately, eighteen thousand million grains per gram. The samples contained many small fragments of rock, so far disintegrated that they went to pieces at once between the fingers, or when they were gently rubbed with the rubber pestle under water. As these fragments would so readily fall to pieces in handling, much of this was classed as "fine earth," and only 17.23 per cent. could be separated out as coarse material. I think that this type has not its true agricultural place in the arrangement of these tables, as the grains of sand and clay have evidently not the same arrangement as in a soil where the disintegration has been more complete and the grains are more evenly distributed. It was stated in a previous section that these soils were naturally poor, but had good body and could be improved. This table shows that they have good body, and it remains now to show how the actual conditions differ from the best conditions which should prevail in this type soil, and how the soils can best be improved. In other States, where these shales are more thoroughly decomposed, they make some of the most fertile lands. They should have a value not far below that of the Helderberg limestone.

There is but a small area of the Helderberg limestone in this State, occurring in several narrow belts crossing Western Maryland. The area of the whole formation is only a few square miles in extent. The formation gives a very fine grass and wheat soil. In the calculations which follow, I have used the Helderberg limestone as the strongest soil, and the best for grass and wheat of any of the types, not having sufficient samples from the Trenton limestone to establish a satisfactory type sample.

I must again urge, as in a former paragraph, that the number of grains of sand and clay give only the skeleton structure of the soil, and that this may be so filled in with organic matter as to greatly modify the physical properties of the soil. The amount of organic matter is assumed to be fairly constant for the different types, and is a matter of more importance in the study of local soils. It is important also to remember that the structure of the soil, and its relation to the circulation of water, is dependent not only upon how many grains there are per gram, but upon how these grains are arranged. In our calculations, we have assumed that they have the same mean arrangement in all the type soils; but this is evidently not so in regard to local soils, for we have suggested that the deterioration of soils is due largely to a change in the arrangement of the soil grains, changing the relation of the soil to the circulation of water. These type samples, however, represent more than this, for they are selected to represent the average, natural condition of these great soil formations.

The average, natural arrangement of the grains in these great soil formations must be determined to give an additional basis of comparison between the different types, but especially for the comparison of local soils, which may have departed, in one way or another, from the type conditions, through a re-arrangement of the grains of sand and clay. This is important in the study and classification of local soils.

It is quite possible to conceive of a brick clay or a tight pipe clay, having no more grains per gram than this Helderberg limestone. If a few drops of caustic ammonia was applied to the Helderberg soil, through which a certain weight of water was passing in a hundred minutes, the grains of soil would be re-arranged, and it would take several thousand minutes for the same amount of water to pass. On the other hand, a little lime water would make the soil more loamy, and hasten the rate of movement of water. We have thus a loam soil, a good clay soil and an impervious pipe clay, out of the same soil, by a simple re-arrangement of the sand and clay. The arrangement of the grains has, therefore, an important bearing on the physical properties of the soil, but this is largely dependent upon local causes, which modify the conditions in the original soil formation.

From the results in these tables it would seem that the subsoil of good grass land would have not less than 30 per cent. of clay, or about *twelve thousand million* grains per gram, and good wheat land not less than twenty per cent., or about *nine thousand million* grains per gram; *provided*, these grains have a certain mean arrangement and that this skeleton structure contains an average amount of organic matter. It must be remembered that if either the arrangement of the grains or the amount and condition of the organic matter departs from the average condition of the soil, the physical condition of the local soil will depart from the typical conditions of the soil formation.

These type subsoils have the following approximate extent of surface area per cubic foot:

276. Pine barrens.	40 per cent. space.	23 940 square feet.	
284. Truck.	45 " " "	74 130 " "	
286. Tobacco.	50 " " "	84 850 " "	
290. Oriskany.	50 " " "	87 720 " " •	
280. Wheat.	55 " " "	94 540 " "	
278. River terrace.	55 " " "	106 200 " "	
282. Triassic.	55 " " "	127 000 " "	
288. Helderberg limestone.	65 " " "	129 700 " "	
238. Catskill.	55 " " "	133 300 " "	
289. Shales (Hamilton, &c.)	60 " " "	142 700 " "	

The practical bearing of these results has been quite fully set forth in Section VIII. The Helderberg limestone has a place here before the Catskill and the shales, because we have given it a high percentage of empty space, higher perhaps than should have been given. It has, of course, the highest percentage of surface area per unit weight of any of these subsoils, but the larger amount of space lowers the percentage per unit volume of soil.

From the foregoing results, we have calculated the relative rate with which a given quantity of water would pass through an equal depth of these subsoils, under a constant force and with the same amount of water (12 per cent.) in each subsoil, taking the subsoil of the Helderberg limestone as a basis of comparison.

It would appear from results on next page that, with 12 per cent. of water present in all the subsoils, it will take only 8 minutes for a quantity of water to pass through the subsoil of the pine barrens, which would require 100 minutes to pass through the same depth of the subsoil of the Helderberg limestone. It will pass through the subsoil of the wheat land of the river terraces in Southern Maryland in about 49 minutes. It will move down more readily in these lighter soils from its own weight, but, as I have urged in a previous section, a given quantity of water could not be raised so readily to supply the needs of a growing crop, for there would be less exposed water-surface to contract, that is, there would be less force to pull it up.

No.	Soil.	Space.	Water-content.	Relative Time.
276.	Pine barrens.	40 per cent.	12 per cent.	8
284.	Truck.	45 " "	12 " "	21
286.	Tobacco.	50 " "	12 " "	33
290.	Oriskany.	50 " "	12 " "	35
280.	Wheat.	55 " "	12 " "	45
278.	River terrace.	55 " "	12 " "	49
282.	Triassic.	55 " "	12 " "	56
238.	Catskill.	55 " "	12 " "	58
289.	Shales (Hamilton, &c.)	60 " "	12 " "	81
288.	Helderberg limestone.	65 " "	12 " "	100

I have calculated the amount of water which should be present in these different subsoils for the rate of movement, due to a constant force, to be the same as in the subsoil of the Helderberg limestone, containing 12 per cent. of water.

No.	Soil.	Space.	Water-content.	Relative Time.
276.	Pine barrens.	40 per cent.	5.3 per cent.	101
284.	Truck.	45 " "	7.2 " "	101
286.	Tobacco.	50 ". "	8.4 " "	102 .
290.	Oriskany.	50 " "	8.6 " "	101
280.	Wheat.	55 " "	9.4 " "	100
278.	River terrace.	55 " "	9.6 " "	100
282.	Triassic.	55 " "	10.0 " "	101
238.	Catskill.	55 " "	10.1 " "	100
289.	Shales (Hamilton, &c.)	60 " "	11.2 " "	100
288.	Helderberg limestone.	65 " "	12.0 " "	100

The relation of these different subsoils to water is as different as in the artificial conditions in green house culture. The difference is amply sufficient to account for the distribution of plants and for the known relations of these different soils to plant growth and development.

I have also calculated the relative rate with which water would move, under a constant force, through these different subsoils, if all the space within them was filled with water.

No.	Soil.	Space.	Water-content.	Relative Time.
276.	Pine barrens.	40 per cent.	20.10 per cent. (sat.)	74
284.	Truck.	45 " "	22.41 " " "	141
286.	Tobacco.	50 " "	27.42 " " "	121
290.	Oriskany.	50 " "	27.42 " " "	130
280.	Wheat.	55 " "	31.55 " " "	109
278.	River terrace.	55 " "	31.55 " " "	119
282.	Triassic.	55 " "	31.55 " " "	137
238.	Catskill.	55 " "	31.55 " " "	140
289.	Shales (Hamilton, &c.)	60 " "	36.14 " " "	123
288.	Helderberg limestone.	65 " "	41.22 " " "	100

It will be seen that the amount of space assigned to these different soil formations, has an important bearing on the relative rate with which water will move within the different soils. The coarser textured soils have less space and will contain less water than the clay soils. The subsoil of the truck land has only 45 per cent. of space, and will hold but 22.41 per cent. by weight of water, when this space is completely filled. The subsoil of the Helderberg limestone has 65 per cent. of space, and will hold 41.22 per cent. by weight of water, or nearly twice as much as the truck land. When the soils contained only 12 per cent. of water, a quantity of water would move through the truck land in 21 minutes, which would require 100 minutes to pass through the subsoil of the Helderberg limestone. When, however, these soils are taxed to their utmost, it will take 141 minutes for a quantity of water to pass through the truck land, which would go through the limestone subsoil in 100 minutes. As suggested in a previous section, this undoubtedly explains a matter of common observation and experience, that crops on these light lands are more injured by excessive wet seasons than crops on heavier soils.

These calculations of the relative rate with which water will move within these different subsoils, are based solely upon the skeleton structure. The influence of the organic matter is not considered, and the soil grains are assumed to have the same mean arrangement. These two factors, the amount of organic matter and the arrangement of the soil grains, are probably nearly alike under the normal conditions which prevail in these great soil formations; but if they have not relatively the same effect in the different soils, they will undoubtedly make the difference in the relation of these soils to the circulation of water, still wider than the values we have assigned. Each of these factors requires a distinct line of investigation, and this is necessary to the practical use and application of this work.

THE SOIL,

CONSIDERED AS A

SEPARATE AND DISTINCT DEPARTMENT OF NATURE,

BY

ROBERT. SERRELL.WOOD,

Corresponding Member of the National Institute.

WASHINGTON, MARCH, 1850.

The most palpable source of nutrition to all created beings was supposed by the ancients to possess the attributes of vitality ; it was therefore an amiable weakness on their part to personify the Earth, and to hold her in peculiar veneration. Modern science has banished this beautiful sentiment from its stern philosophy, but it can never invalidate the fact that there are certain ingredients of the soil (whatever be their origin) which claim intermediate rank between matter in such states of combination as the chemist can produce by synthesis, and the lowest specimens of vegetable organisms : neither has it yet successfully proved that the same elements in other shape than the organic salts of humus contribute with equal efficiency to the luxuriance of vegetation, although there is evidence in volcanic and other localities to show, that an excess of either free carbonic acid gas, or ammonia, or water, even when the other minerals present suffice for the wants of plants, is injurious to the highest degree. A greater proportion than at present of those gases and vapours in the atmosphere, and consequently in the soil, may have favored the earliest denizens of our globe : those tribes have now nearly passed away, or their constitution has been modified with modifications of climate, &c.

A just appreciation of fossil organic remains has elicited a probable truth, that function and organization proceed through both kingdoms of nature by parallel lines of advancement, observable since the different periods of the world at which they respectively commenced their existence. It would seem as if some general law, harmonizing with the earth's progress in its physical capacity, governed the succession of these products, an idea which is further supported by their gradual development at the present day from the germinal to a perfect state. We should also bear in mind the remarkable fact, that animals and vegetables are blended together so as to render any attempt to define their distinguishing properties utterly futile. Vegeto-animals have been fully recognised by naturalists; and we are next led to inquire whether the soil, forming a connection between organized and unorganized matter, partakes of a *vegeto-mineral* character in the highest acceptation of the term.

The animal department, although indebted for its growth and prime condition to azotized aliment approximating more or less in its nature the tissues themselves, borrows, from vegetables especially, hydro-carbonaceous substances of a less complex composition, a portion of which is converted into fat, another portion is directly oxidized and excreted, while a third is presumed, in the case of the lowest animals, to be convertible by means of ammonia into gelatine, &c., their integuments corresponding with those of plants as surfaces absorbent of nourishment, sufficiently at least to establish a close relation between both races in this respect as well as in their both inhaling oxygen.* Again, the vegetable department in its highest range, although dependant upon rich mould or organic manures for its most efficient support, (as man and some other animals are upon flesh,) draws from the atmosphere elements convertible into cellulose, &c., indicating the claims of animals upon vegetables, of vegetables upon the soil, and, as I shall endeavor to show, the ultimate dependance of the soil upon the atmosphere. Nature evidently proposes more than one resource for the maintenance of her creatures; and unity of design, which pervades the works of creation, would suggest that, although the soil receives its most unequivocal accessions from the debris of plants, it nevertheless allows the crude materials of air to circulate within its pores, and to form more notable combinations. Animals, vegetables, and the soil are constituted in large proportion of particles, which have possessed, but which no longer retain, the usual characteristics of life—particles, be it observed, which threaten to resolve themselves into simpler forms, unless the tendency to disintegration be

---

*The oxidation of the hydrocarburets is generally believed to liberate caloric in living bodies as a primary result, but I respectfully maintain that it, in the first instance, causes the surrender of electricity which was previously combined; heat consequently becomes a secondary effect of an altered consistency or composition in solids or fluids, whereby their specific capacity for caloric is affected. The temperature of animals is exaggerated by physical exertion, which causes the contraction of muscles and a more rapid circulation of the blood. A large portion of their food is already combined with oxygen in the proportion to form water; no heat is therefore evolved from this source, and the separation of free water from their surfaces in the shape of vapour produces a reduction of temperature perhaps equivalent to the heat generated by the conversion of venous into arterial blood. The slow reactions between highly constituted substances may be identical in a chemical point of view with ordinary cases of combustion, but the results very different; the amount of heat liberated being proportionate to the greater or less competency of conducting media to carry off the electricity set free, or of other contiguous molecules in the circulation or elsewhere to appropriate that imponderable by forming new combinations. And here I may be permitted to add, that if the solution of a simple metal in the voltaic apparatus liberates a force which, on being conducted by a special arrangement of wire around an enclosed bar of iron, *magnetizes it, a fortiori* the resolution of more complex particles, such as those contained in the animal circulation, might be supposed capable of contracting (magnetizing) a muscle enclosed within a network of conducting nervous filaments. A ganglion is the voltaic apparatus, certain constituents of the blood electrolytes, the motor and sensitive nerves conducting media, and the muscle, which is insulated by cellular matter and ligament, a magnet. The contraction of a muscle or a congeries of muscles would not necessarily diminish the volume of their mass, because their reduction of size only tends to enlarge the capacity of the surrounding cellular substance; free ingress is therefore allowed to the blood between the fibres, and consequently greater efficiency produced in the parts.

counteracted by a force of an opposite kind. The soil possesses no evidence of organization either in mass or in detail ; but organization may mark grades of development without being indispensable to characterize living matter. Nothing can be more indefinite than even the essential properties of life. Can physiologists determine at what precise moment the vital principle is surrendered by a piece of muscle cut from the leg of a healthy animal ? The separation of a part merely shortens its term of existence by destroying perhaps the faculty of self-preservation or reproduction. Where then shall we find the first link in the self-supporting chain of vital products ? Are we to consider the vesicles or cells which the microscope discovers almost everywhere on the earth's surface as exhibiting the simplest manifestations of life, or may we refer its rudiments to the corpuscles of blood, or to certain constituents of sap ?

I propose to regard the soil as a creature *sui generis*, sustaining living bodies whilst it is itself sustained by them. Its proportions are limited by the means of increment placed at its disposal. If the natural history of soil be studied, we find that although it may increase enormously under certain conditions, and although its term of maturity may be prolonged to an apparently indefinite extent, its ultimate dissolution, in whole or in part, is a matter of as much certainty as the lapse of ages. Organized bodies, however, display their power of increase more particularly in their progeny, which represent the parent in an enlarged individuality. The soil, likewise constituted, as I shall presently endeavor to show, of many individuals of different character, is capable of propagating its kind by a quasi-fissiparous process—that is to say, a portion of veritable mould being isolated from the main body and placed in a favorable situation, exerts a quickening influence upon surrounding matter of elemental identity: mould, consequently, either enlarges in bulk itself, or gives bulk to vegetables, just as vegetables, during their growth, either enlarge in bulk themselvs, or give bulk to animals which feed upon them. It may be further urged, as a general proposition, that animals, plants, and the soil, increase and multiply in co-ordinate ratios, and that, with the continued addition of light, a much greater mass of matter will be engaged in the enjoyment of more exalted faculties, either in an organized or semi-organized shape.

Aboriginal soil, then, may be attributed to the rays of the sun co-operating with physical changes of certain universally diffused substances, which I shall presently mention—changes of form, consistency, and position, capable of impressing the heterogeneous residue with new affinities. We, however, regard, as *chiefly instrumental*, at the present day, in the generation of *humus de novo* from carbonic acid and water, *the forces liberated by already existing humus, or by materials of higher grade in the act of decomposition*—forces identical with those emitted from the luminous worlds around us.

Commencing with the lowest grade of progressive developments, we submit for consideration : first, whether ulmin and other semi-organized substances were not originally, and are not still, produced from carbonic acid and water. at the expense of ammonia which becomes decomposed in the ground by means of oxygen, nitrogen being liberated upon the same terms which vegetables prescribe for themselves during an analogous process of transformation.* Secondly, whether the disintegration of those hydrocarburets which are formed in vegetables from ulmin, such as starch, gums, oils, &c., does not promote the formation of various azotized proximate principles, when ammonia, sulphur, phosphorus, and some few other minerals, are present. Lastly, whether the dissolution of these proteine and allied compounds into less complex forms, or into their ultimate elements, does not generate cellulose, &c. The idea on which we particularly insist is, the reluctance on the part of bodies, whether organized or unorganized, to allow their constitutional forces to exhaust themselves by their component materials becoming resolved into simpler combinations, as long as contiguous matter evinces the disposition of assuming an identical character or an equivalent complexity of constitution. For this reason, the same forces which enter into the constitution of vegetables are apparently transmitted from one generation to another. But, on the other hand, it must be confessed that, were it not for the incessant appropriations of the luminous element by the surface materials of our globe, no further progress in the quantity or quality of chemico-vital phenomena could be anticipated.

It would likewise be unreasonable to expect the occurrence of these spontaneous formations of soil, where the want of indispensable prerequisites prohibits what would be an ordinary train of events in more favored regions. The fixed alkalies and ~~alkaloids~~, in moderate quantity, might expedite the process, and yet the same bases, or ammonia, or water, in excess, effectually prevent it. To consider them as tending to break up, under all circumstances, rather than to superinduce more complex relations of matter, would be to adopt an error equivalent with considering oxygen an element of universal destruction.

Viewed solely as an accumulation of dead or effete materials, the ground presents a melancholy picture of desolation, but as a thing of life it offers eminent support to the doctrine of development. As soon as a fit habitation was prepared for land-animals and plants, they each in the fulness of time entered on their career. There is an aptitude in this arrangement, and no less probable is it that the first and simplest forms of living matter derived their forces from existing substances of lower degree in complexity, and that the light of heaven co-operated then, as it does now, in the glorious consummation. Water-plants flourished long before dry land appeared; these must have subsisted upon gases and salts dissolved in the ocean, and their debris became the source of much primeval soil. This admission by no means militates against the proposition that semi-organized compounds, constituting humus, may also be formed in Nature's laboratory by a direct union of the elements concerned, the most obvious cause of a primary character being the reduction of ammonia, or its transformation, into water and nitrogen, by means of oxygen. Whether other compounds be formed in the soil, such as nitrates, which are due to progressive as well as retrograde re-

---

* It may be observed that the gaseous effluvia (excretions proper) respired by the leaves of plants, are for the most part simple elements, as oxygen and nitrogen, which, on assuming the aeriform condition, give up the electricity previously binding them with solids in the closest chemical relations; their loss of this force redounds to the benefit of plants by the consequent fixation of carbon.

actions, must depend upon dynamic contingencies. Holding these premises in mind, we are led to inquire whether the decomposition of semi-organized compounds did not liberate the necessary forces and introduce the lowest types of vegetable organisms, under conditions of the world more favorable than at present, and which we can scarcely now appreciate.* These in turn becoming decomposed, and surrendering their forces, may have forwarded new combinations of vegetable matter, until we reach a period of the earth's history teeming with vital phenomena familiar to us.

Germs, like nuclei of lesser note, may be identical, or nearly so, in their ultimate or proximate elements, and yet differ in the proportions of their combined imponderables. On this hypothesis the variety of vegetables and even animals is divested somewhat of mystery; the elements of nutrition being the same, the congenital forces which direct the earliest vital movements in each particular genus or species determine their subsequent figure and organization.

After making due allowance for climate and the immediate effects of solar irradiation upon the digestive powers of plants, we attach no little importance to the shape in which their food is presented to the roots. It is asserted by the modern school of Agricultural Chemists, that the organic food of plants is exclusively carbonic acid and ammonia dissolved in water, and, of course, the force of life is esteemed the chief cause of all organic changes of a progressive character. With us, on the contrary, it is contended, that the substances aforesaid could not possibly be metamorphosed into higher compounds except by the addition of light, or of forces identical with light, derived from organized and semi-organized materiel in the act of decomposition. It is well known, that no manure is more acceptable to vegetables than their own decaying leaves, or the debris of a higher class of plants; the explanation now offered for this fact by authors entitled to our utmost respect, is, as stated above, very simple; but unfortunately it leaves the solution of ulterior phenomena hopeless. To attribute the more abstruse transmutations to a force of life is tantamount to an abandonment of principles applicable to all

* These conditions have reference to former bipolar movements of our earth, not of an extravagant, but of an exaggerated kind. I intend, on some future occasion, to submit reasons for the belief that the sun is the immediate cause of the diurnal rotation of planets within the solar system, and of their annual changes of position and presentation. To be more explicit: if solar rays be compounded, as I shall argue, of repellent and attractive forces neutralized by their combination in light, and they be decomposed on the surface of the earth, (this surface being a mixed one of solids, liquids, and aeriform fluids,) we can understand how more of the calorific rays may be detained on the peripheral or outer portion of our planet, and exert an influence there, while the electric rays, for the most part, pass on to the innermost surface of the solid crust, causing additional layers to be precipitated from the central fluid mass. A temporary loss of equilibrium thus occasioned between the opposite sides of the sphere, produces a centrifugal tendency in the comparatively enlarged proximal surface, and a centripetal tendency in the distal surface, which becomes, each section of it for the instant, comparatively smaller than its antipod. We further surmise that the earth has reached its present rate of movement and extent of bipolar oscillation after considerable diminution of intensity in the North and South hemispheres respectively, at different epochs; that the approaches to a more perfect equilibrium and consequent alterations of climate from this cause, have been so gradual within the historic period as to have escaped the notice of observers in this field of science. I am not acquainted with any more plausible explanation of the undoubted changes of level in the ocean since the commencement of the tertiary era, as evidenced by phenomena of universal extent.

physical changes for the production of which chemists are unable to control or concentrate the usual forces of matter.

Practical agriculturists will ~~hesitate before they discard the ancient belief~~ that proximate principles must be, and in all cases are, reduced before they can be absorbed by the roots. Because analytical chemists are unable to dissolve by artificial means divers ingredients of humus, it does not follow that a force derived from the voltaic movements of contiguous living tissues is incompetent to do so; neither does it follow that the constituents of the ascending sap vessels, or of animal chyliferous ducts, represent matter in its identical form as appropriated from the primæ viæ, or the soil, because the organic portions of food may become attached to the presenting superficial tissues, before the force of absorption separates and reduces them to other soluble compounds as found in the sap and chylous lymph. Although I have contended that the precipitation of the solids in living bodies is mainly due to forces derived from analogous materials, yet accretions to the roots of plants probably occur at all seasons; during spring and summer, however, the foliage enjoys the privilege of appropriating aeriform food by means of light, in addition to the forces borrowed from chemical and mechanical reactions.

The usual articles of food correspond more or less with the tissues which prevail in living bodies; hence it happens that, when referring to animals, practical as well as speculative agriculturists lay great stress upon fibrin, albumen, phosphate of lime, &c.; when referring to plants they formerly paid especial regard to the ordinary ingredients of humus, and while pursuing that natural system (apart from the use of highly stimulating manures, both organic and inorganic) were not troubled with the treatment or the discussion of modern vegetable diseases. We now suspect that just as there are peculiar principles in vegetables which produce constitutional effects on animals, so there are in vegetable mould of good quality combinations, not the result merely of decomposition, but of direct union between the elements concerned; and that these vegeto-mineral varieties are of great importance, and define the nicer qualifications of soil and consequent character of plants cultivated therein. The nervous matter of animals taken as food appears most likely to sustain the nervous system and to promote the growth of neurine within our own frames. No people feeding on vegetables exclusively has ever attained eminence in the scale of nations; not because neurine cannot be formed from vegetable products, but because it cannot be so bountifully formed. However much disposed the digestive apparatus may be to reduce the ingesta to a homogeneous fluid, certain substances pass its ordeal which may eventually give flavor, color, and other characteristics to both animals and vegetables.* Public opinion has changed even in respect to the elements which necessarily enter into the composition of

---

*A very general repugnance to truck raised upon night-soil exists, and I believe the objections are to a certain extent valid. When vegetables are supplied with but a moderate amount of such offensive manure, the probability is, that the digestive powers of the roots will completely alter the character of such portions of food as are not assimilated by the soil; or even if any is directly absorbed into the vegetable system, it is very rapidly decomposed and passed away. The case is different when plants are rendered rank and stimulated by an excess of sewage; and it is from such an unnatural and continuous process of forcing growth that we instinctively revolt.

vegetables, but is still adverse to an acknowledgement of any advan-
tage derivable from the direct absorption of compounds highly endowed.
We cannot detect any absolute contrast in kind, such as is alleged to
exist, between the materials constituting the food of animals and vegetables, but simply a difference in amount of semi-organized and mineral nutriment appropriated by the races respectively, corresponding with
their functions and the complexity of their organisms. The fungous and
certain parasitic tribes establish this view of the subject almost conclu-
sively. Light is necessary to their health and welfare in different degrees; its influence upon the functions of the human body being small,
there is the greater necessity for man's securing a full supply of proteinized aliment, and a moderate allowance of those vegetable stimulants
and beverages which administer to his gratification. It is in vain to
shut our eyes to what some may consider a humiliatory fact, that diet
essentially contributes to our physical and mental calibre.

From these miscellaneous data we infer that, although humus consists mainly of well-known organic matter, it contains other substances
which perform an office entirely overlooked by agriculturists, and ad-
monishes them to reconsider the necessity of frequent rotations in crops,
so far as permanent improvement of the soil, and not immediate profit
by overtaxing its every capability, is concerned. The staples of a country, being ascertained by experience, may be encouraged by strictly res-
toring to the ground the refuse of those staples as specific manure. The
minute products referred to exhibit to my mind degrees of chemico-vital
complexity and corresponding differences in their physiological relations.
Not the least reason, perhaps, why the cerealia in particular are disin-
clined to extreme climates, or certain regions of country in even temperate
latitudes, is the same which prevented them from sooner gracing the bosom
of our earth, to wit, the want or insufficiency of appropriate semi-organized aliment. I may be told that grain has been successfully raised without the least portion of humus, or any of this highly-extolled materia ali-
mentaria. We will join issue on this point, and await the verdict of good
and true men, who will weigh the evidence of unexceptionable and long-
continued experiments; and if the cerealia do not degenerate or become
diseased, as potatoes have become, by the injudicious refinements of art,
I shall be agreeably disappointed. There cannot, I suspect, be too great a
supply of mould if there be also a proper proportion of mineral ingredients, and silica in particular, to support the luxuriant stem. While
calculating the value of this class of plants we should be mindful not
to underrate the straw, whether as food, litter, or manure, for domestic
consumption. The tuber of potatoes has been perhaps over-stimulated
by unfermented organic manures not possessing a sufficiency of mineral
bases to ensure hardy germs; whereas, what seems to threaten wheat is
an excess of inorganic elements over the organic, so as to render
it eventually more grain than stem ; and thus by forcing year after year
exuberant seed and a precocious progeny, we endanger the permanent
welfare of the plant. It is true that the grain crops are not cultivated
for their leaves or roots, as cabbages or turnips are; but does not the
constitution of the germ depend upon the efficiency of the parent's whole
structure ? The evil is analogous to that of *breeding in and in*, whereby

certain organs, peculiar products, and morbid tendencies are exaggera‑
ted to the prejudice of the other parts and functions. Such a system
must terminate disastrously to animals and vegetables, as it operates
injuriously to the healthy condition and growth of humus, when by re‑
peated over-doses of any one element, or by the total neglect of others,
or by allowing certain noxious elements to accumulate, we depress the
productive energies of the soil.

An argument is frequently raised in disparagement of mould, that an
excess of vegetable matter, as in swamps or heath-moors, is unfavor‑
able to a wholesome vegetation : on the other hand, experiments have
proved that certain plants will thrive in pure charcoal—plants which do
not deserve to be styled useful except by indirection, transplanted from
rich garden earth, containing abundant resources in their systems, sup‑
plied freely with water perhaps saturated with organic matter, in a
close atmosphere charged with concentrated nutriment, in a green-house
which collects the rays of the sun with great effect upon growth ; plants
such as these, many of which cannot survive a sudden change of tem‑
perature, and die out or are forgotten in a few generations, are brought
in comparison with field crops, t e support of man and his fortunes !
It may not be inappropriate, by way of comparison, to direct my readers
to those conditions of society in which a pampered aristocracy is found
in juxta-position with a degraded, ignorant, and vicious populace : the
former are the hot-house plants, the latter those noisome weeds which
from their very rankness are cumbersome to the ground. Happy is
that country in which neither class exists, but a population of intelligent
freemen, with such qualifications of mind and body as ennoble the race.

As far as plants administer to the food of men and domestic animals,
their importance may be graduated by the amount of their fecula, gum,
oils, &c., or of albumen, &c. In order to obtain these products the plants
are generally destroyed, some of them in embryo as seeds and tubers,
some more advanced in life : but we never wait until these latter sponta‑
neously cease to live, because at the period of their natural dissolution
their hydro-carbonaceous deposites have been converted into lignin. The
proteinized deposites in the cells and nitrogenous solutions in the sap
have also disappeared ; they have done their appropriate duty, which
partly corresponds with that performed by the adipose deposites in the
cellular substance of animals, or by the fatty matters of bile. Vegeta‑
bles, with a view to their self-preservation, are known to use the hydro‑
carbonaceous substances in their sap for building up their structures, at the
same time borrowing, as I conceive, the necessary forces from the azotic
ingredients, until the germs divert the juices measurably from the stem
and branches. In consideration of the collateral uses of azotized matter in
vegetables we are too apt to regard it as forming an integral portion
of a plant *per se*. The vegetable and vegeto-mineral kingdoms economize
nitrogen, not for its own sake, but for the advantageous reactions which
it promotes : the vegeto-animal and animal kingdoms appropriate hydro‑
carburets chiefly for that purpose. The same principle may be extended
to their modes of growth at the incipient stage of their existence ; phane‑
rogamous flowering plants not being fecundated until the pollen reaches
the blossom, nor the animal ovum until the semen masculinum quickens it.

9

The very compound ammonia which under favorable circumstances, such as an abundance of carbonaceous aliment, might forward the growth of plants, under other circumstances becomes the means of disintegrating their frame-work even unto utter debility and death. It is for this reason I deprecate an excessive use of, or an entire dependence upon, the fertilizing salts now so prevalent, which will probably cause a more rapid exhaustion of the soil unless we keep our farms in good heart ; and *then* we may lay on the minerals with a liberal hand. Thus are true economy and high tillage combined. Our interest demands that we foster the carbonaceous elements of the soil on the Atlantic slope of this continent, in order to compete with the middle States of the West, notwithstanding the diseases of new countries which affect both animals and vegetables : nearly all of them will soon be avoided by scientific and careful husbandry, more particularly by draining. The refuse of our homesteads and green manures must be our chief resource, and in proportion as we gain carbon by any available means, we should encourage its still further accumulation by an equivalent admixture of mineral bases, among which ammonia is pre-eminently serviceable, both as a solvent or vehicle, and as a stimulant in the manner suggested.

In reply to those who consider the atmosphere competent to supply a full amount of carbon both to the leaves and roots of our field and garden crops, and who, conformably with this doctrine, rely upon mineral manures, I would ask why the ammonia which is furnished in the same way does not suffice. Can the vapor of water dissolved in air, or even the dew which is deposited at night, sustain under ordinary circumstances the welfare of the higher class of vegetables for a season, not to mention a series of years ? It might as well be contended that no rain is needed anywhere, because in Egypt the periodical overflow of the Nile renders it unnecessary *there* by soaking the adjacent plains to an extraordinary depth, as that wheat can be raised on poor soil for many successive years without the slightest artificial or natural additions of carbon in some of its solid or liquid forms.

We do not propose adding compounds of nitrogen to worn-out soil solely for the purpose of raising vegetable mould, although the improvement in the soil is the first step in the improvement of our vegetables, and consequently of our animals. Whether our increase of wealth consist of azotized food which has been acquired at the expense of hydro-carbonaceous matter in vegetables, or whether it consists of hydro-carbonaceous organizable matter in the soil which has been acquired at the expense of ammoniacal ingredients, the chemical process is identical ; and when the value of good mould is taken into account, the difference between the market prices of the organized and semi-organized products is not always in favor of the first.

During the decomposition of a manure heap or a compost bed, as long as ammoniacal fumes escape, provided the air be allowed to percolate the mass, and there be no deficiency of fixed alkalies and alkaline earths, I fully believe that a positive addition of semi-organized substances results; although the retention of ammonia is doubly desirable for direct appropriation by growing plants, a desideratum, which may be in some measure effected by artificial means. Were, however, the loss of ammonia complete, which it generally is not, the porous character of the new-born mould would attract back again a certain proportion. Thus it happens that as in the atmosphere, carbonic acid, ammonia, and vapor, hold a proportionate relation to each other, so do they in the soil near the surface of the ground, and it is in consequence of the natural inability of the mineral bases to regulate their own movements satisfactorily in reference to vegetation, that man is called upon to remedy any defects or excesses. It is usually asserted by those who admit the supply of carbonic acid and ammonia to the roots from decaying organic matter, that the atmosphere was the primeval source of those elements; they therefore refer the origin of vegetables or vegetable growth to that vast magazine, as amply empowered to sustain what it originated. We admit the joint influence of gases, liquids, and solids on living bodies, and this we hold to be sufficient to account for all the material phenomena and reactions of life.

Whether this theory be right or wrong, no injury can accrue from the adoption of a practice founded on its requirements. We should by no means place our sole reliance upon the natural but slow formations of soil as food for our cultivated crops, any more than we should rely upon the organic elements of the atmosphere, or of the same elements absorbed by ground kept in fine tilth. For precisely similar reasons we should object to feeding our domestic animals upon food slightly azotized, if our aim be to gain flesh and nerve. Under favorable conditions then, and by the aid of light, the pulverized surface of worn-out soil becomes slowly self-renovated, provided its texture be porous and yet sufficiently retentive; and this recuperation proceeds the more rapidly in proportion to the amount of semi-organized substances already existing. A nucleus assists, without being necessary to, formative action. We may not at first, or at once, attain a pabulum adapted to sweet vegetation; indeed we might never succeed without slight extraneous additions. I therefore do not recommend any purely natural system of agriculture for civilized communities; but as a question of physiology, I contend, that as a coarse vegetation precedes the development of nobler plants, so the commonest earthy bases, in conjunction with water and the elements of the atmosphere, serve to prepare poor land for future usefulness, by a succession of higher and higher subterranean products; and among the elements of air I include phosphorus, sulphur, and some other minerals, either in solution or mechanically suspended.

It is, moreover, questionable, whether the organic acids in combination with mineral bases, or other still more abundant ~~organic substances the~~ constituents proper of soil, are so unstable as generally supposed; a doubt which may be extended to the constituents proper of living vegetables and animals, as long as easily-decomposable matters in the circulation or otherwise favorably located, are available for functional purposes; whether, for instance, the exposure of those hydrocarburets to the atmosphere, by repeated fallows, necessarily entails their speedy loss in the absence or comparative paucity of growing plants; the latter alternative, of course, resulting in no necessary loss, provided the plants be allowed to rot on the ground or within the furrow. My own impression is, that under the circumstances stated, and as long as moisture is maintained, partial decomposition is adequately compensated by ~~original carbonized formations~~, these again to be supplanted in natural order by original hydrocarbonaceous deposites at the expense of the atmosphere. Uncropped land which has been kept constantly worked for several successive seasons, or which has been lying waste for five or ten years, may be gradually accumulating vegeto-mineral products peculiar to the climate, to such an extent that the application of a little guano alone will ensure a remunerating crop of grain. This is no argument in disproof of my main position, for I have uniformly discovered that, where the ground was decidedly worthless and bare, the whole class of mineral manures disappointed me; but where a scanty allowance of humus gave them a chance of turning that pittance to immediate account, the crop spoke for itself, if the season was favorable; although, as I have before remarked, it was tasking the ground to its utmost strength for the purpose of giving the crop a good start.

The constitutional depravity of the middle regions in Maryland and Virginia must be assigned to the exhaustion of available alkalies and alkaline earths, and to the too rapid withdrawal of sulphur and phosphorus. Let the proper mineral bases bear the right proportion in a raw surface composed of rock lately disintegrated, and if the climate be genial, there can be little doubt of a soil-formation, and subsequent vegetation based upon it, even on a solitary island in the midst of the Atlantic ocean.

The conclusion to which we arrive is, that animals, vegetables, and the soil hold certain properties in common, alike affecting their growth and the means of obtaining nutriment. When circumstances admit, they all appropriate materials but little if at all removed in composition from their own substance; but they also are enabled to generate within their system more or less compounds suitable to their immediate wants from the same elements in simpler states of combination. The more capital, therefore, we judiciously invest in organic manures, or in mineral manures with a view of fostering humus, the more deeply we plough and pulverize the soil within prudential limits, the larger interest accrues, not only by the increased weight and quality of produce above ground, but also below the surface.

MOUNT HERMON, WASHINGTON COUNTY, *March*, 1850.

www.ingramcontent.com/pod-product-compliance
Lightning Source LLC
Chambersburg PA
CBHW021530090426
42739CB00007B/861